Chris Wood

BOEING 747
Operating an Icon

There are many ways to describe the Boeing 747 airliner, good looking, well-made, with high performance and oodles of passenger comfort. Since the first 747 aircraft made the type's maiden flight from Everett-Paine Field Washington, the aircraft has captured the hearts of people from around the world. Today the Boeing 747 is broadly regarded as an icon. There are others. Concorde is revered for its elegance and supersonic capabilities, but only 20 were built, it carried up to 120 passengers, each of whom had to be wealthy to afford a ticket. The Airbus A380 is admired for its gargantuan size, so big it was dubbed the Super Jumbo, 251 were built, and it typically carried up to 575 passengers.

Icon or not, the Boeing 747 was a winner for Boeing in many ways. Production ran from 1968 until early 2023 during which time 1,574 were built. For airlines, the 747 offered favourable operating costs and capacity, the 300, 400, and 8 series carried more than 400 passengers or long-haul routes all over the world. For airports, the 747 brought thousands of passengers through the doors and fitted the existing infrastructure with few exceptions. For passengers, and not just wealthy ones, the 747 revolutionised air travel in terms of affordability and comfort. If you were a passenger on a 747 you may well have appreciated both factors and more.

Today of course, the 747 has largely given way to new generation of wide-body twinjets equipped with more fuel-efficient engines. Whilst not as cabin roomy as the 747, new generation airliners need to offer affordability

and passenger comfort, which they do. But they are not quite like flying on a jumbo!

Plenty of 747s continue to fly, mostly as freighters tasked with carrying goods, that we all enjoy, around the world. As a freighter, the 747 offers a massive load-carrying capability in a gargantuan cargo cabin.

This publication focuses on the people of the 747, those essential to the successful operation of the type - the flight crew, cabin crew, loadmasters and maintainers that operated and continue to operate the jumbo. Whatever your interest in aviation, this much anticipated edition *Operating an Icon: The Boeing 747*, provides many insider stories of the most recognised airliner in the world.

Editor

CONTENTS

Chris Wood

Boeing

Chris Wood

Cargolux

ISBN: 978 1 80282 977 8
Editor: Mark Ayton
Senior editor, specials: Roger Mortimer
Email: roger.mortimer@keypublishing.com
Cover Design: Steve Donovan
Design: SJmagic DESIGN SERVICES, India
Advertising Sales Manager: Sam Clark
Email: sam.clark@keypublishing.com
Tel: 01780 755131
Advertising Production: Becky Antoniades
Email: Rebecca.antoniades@keypublishing.com

SUBSCRIPTION/MAIL ORDER
Key Publishing Ltd, PO Box 300, Stamford, Lincs, PE9 1NA
Tel: 01780 480404
Subscriptions email: subs@keypublishing.com
Mail Order email: orders@keypublishing.com
Website: www.keypublishing.com/shop

PUBLISHING
Group CEO and Publisher: Adrian Cox

Published by
Key Publishing Ltd, PO Box 100, Stamford, Lincs, PE9 1XQ
Tel: 01780 755131
Website: www.keypublishing.com

PRINTING
Precision Colour Printing Ltd, Haldane, Halesfield 1, Telford, Shropshire. TF7 4QQ

DISTRIBUTION
Seymour Distribution Ltd, 2 Poultry Avenue, London, EC1A 9PU
Enquiries Line: 02074 294000.

Introducing the BOEING 747

A brief overview of the Boeing 747 aircraft, the variants, its production factory, and the man that led the design team responsible for this most majestic of aircraft.

Boeing 747-100 testbed N7470 (c/n 20235), the first 747 built on take-off from Everett-Paine Field. *Boeing*

"Boeing's fifth and final series of jumbo aircraft was the 747-8. Two variants were built, the 747-8F freighter and the passenger carrying 747-8I intercontinental."

BOEING 747 PRODUCTION TOTALS BY VARIANT

Variant	Launched	Service Entry	Total	Engine Options	MTOW	Freighter versions
747-100 testbed		Boeing flight test, September 30, 1968	1	JTD9D	Not applicable	Not applicable
747-100	1966	Pan Am 1970	205	CF6, JT9D or RB211	750,000lb	100(SF)
747SP	1975	Pan Am 1976	45	CF6, JT9D or RB211	696,000lb	None
747-200	1968	KLM February 1971	393	CF6, JT9D or RB211	833,000lb	200F, 200C, 200M
747-300	1980	Swissair March 1983	81	CF6, JT9D or RB211	833,000lb	300M
747-400	1985	Northwest Airlines February 1989	694	CF6, PW4000 or RB211	910,000lb	400F, 400BCF, 400ERF
747-8	2005	Cargolux 747-8F October 2011	155	GEnx-2B	987,000lb	8F
Total			1,574			

Joe Sutter joined the Boeing Airplane Company after serving in the US Navy during World War Two. A graduate of aeronautical engineering from the University of Washington in Seattle, his home city, Joe worked on the Boeing 707, 727, 737 and the 747. It was the 747 that Joe Sutter is most closely associated with, primarily because of his job as chief engineer and design team manager throughout its concept, design, and production phases. Sutter continued to work for Boeing until 1986 when he retired as executive vice president for commercial airplane engineering and product development.

The 747's home is Boeing's Everett Factory which is adjacent to Paine Field Airport, some 24 miles north of Seattle. Built in 1967 specifically to house the Boeing 747 production line, by volume, the entire factory is the largest building in the world at 472.3ft³ or 13.3m³.

Given the 747's tail height of 63ft and the need for plenty of headroom over the production floor so that any of the numerous overhead cranes can lift large components into place, it is small wonder that the building measures 114ft in height. The factory is built immediately adjacent to a main road, aptly named the Boeing Freeway, from where anyone who cares to do so, can drive by the entire length of the factory. The drive provides the onlooker with the chance to marvel at its size, there are six massive hangar doors, each 82ft wide, each painted with a mural coloured in different shades of Boeing's corporate blue.

The first Boeing 747-100 testbed N7470 (c/n 20235) was rolled-out of the building on September 30, 1968. Since that milestone day, the Everett Production Factory has produced thousands of widebody jetliners, 747s, 767s, 777s, and 787s. Today the factory produces 777s and KC-46 tanker aircraft (a military derivative of the 767), which like all the other jets built on the site and towed across a purpose-built bridge over Boeing Freeway to an area that includes engine, fuel and paint facilities used to prepare the aircraft for its first flight and handover to the delivery centre.

Since the roll-out of the testbed aircraft, Boeing has designed and built five main series of 747 aircraft.

DASH EIGHTS

Boeing's fifth and final series of jumbo aircraft was the 747-8. Two variants were built, the 747-8F freighter and the passenger carrying 747-8I intercontinental. Cargolux was the first airline to place an 8-series into revenue earning service with its first 747-8F in October 2011. Lufthansa followed, when its first 747-8I entered revenue earning service in May 2012.

Boeing introduced several enhancements to the 8-series, the most notable being a reduction in the type's operating empty weight (OEW), meaning 747-8 aircraft built later in the type's production run were 9,000lb (4,082kg) lighter than the first examples to roll-out of the Everett factory. Weight was reduced by making hundreds of small changes to the airframe and by improvements in the production and assembly processes, for example, by using sealants less liberally.

A second major enhancement was a 3.5% reduction in fuel burn, 2% of which came from

Boeing 747-8F N863GT (c/n 67150) parked outside the Everett Production Factory on January 31, 2023, when Boeing celebrated delivery of this, the last 747 built, to Atlas Air. The bridge used to tow aircraft across Boeing Freeway can be seen in the top left of the photo. *Boeing*

a Performance Improvement Package (PIP) on the GEnx-2B engine introduced in December 2013. The PIP incorporated a redesigned low-pressure turbine, high-pressure compressor, and an improved combustor. The PIP also included reactivation of the horizontal tank fuel system in the 747-8I which boosted that variant's design range from the initial 7,700 to 8,000 nautical miles.

The 9,000lb OEW reduction accounted for some of the remaining 1.5% improvement; the rest came from subtle changes to the aircraft's aerodynamic profile. These included an outboard aileron bias to optimise the span load of the wing for even airflow distribution all the way to the wing tip, and minor corrections applied to the elevator and rudder to enhance their performance.

Boeing also upgraded the 8-series' flight management computer (FMC) which enables wind and fuel burn data to be uploaded in real time and includes advisories posted about optimum altitude based on current wind conditions, not just on predictions. The upgraded FMC also enabled the pilot to fly the latest navigational approaches, including using the global positioning landing system for very precise arrivals.

The FMC upgrades involved changes to make the -8's climb and cruise performance more efficient. At the time, Bruce Dickinson, vice president and chief project engineer for the 747 programme said: "We've made small

adjustments to make it operationally friendly for flight crews, basically ensuring the features were always available to the flight crews in every circumstance, in other words [that] there weren't fault messages that would prevent that information from being available. It was about enabling trouble-free operations, savings and availability."

Boeing 747-8 aircraft received a 330-minute Extended Operations (ETOPS) Federal Aviation Administration approval. This was the first time a four-engine aircraft received this type of design approval, up from the previous 180 minutes clearance. The 330 ETOPS rating allows operators to fly long distances more directly on virtually any worldwide city pair routing.

The 747-8's flight deck features a vertical situation display (VSD), which presents a profile view of the aircraft's vertical position relative to the predicted flight path and terrain. The VSD also assists with landings, which according to Boeing "reduces the likelihood of missed approaches, rejected landings and runway excursions or overruns."

Another flight deck feature with the 747-8 is commonality with Boeing's electronic flight bag, a tablet device which provides a paperless cockpit with electronic checklists, real-time fault reporting to ground operations centres, and performance calculations.

Most 8-series aircraft in operation are freighters. The 747-8F has a cavernous volume for cargo of 30,288ft³ (857m³) between the main and lower decks. There are 34 positions for 8 x 10ft (2.4 x 3m) contoured pallets on the main deck and 12 positions on the lower deck, where there is also space for two additional LD1 or LD3 containers. Cargolux, the launch customer for the 747-8F

> "The jumbo was overtaken in fulfilling many airlines' high-capacity, long-range needs. This was reflected by the diverging sales fortunes of the 777 and 747 over the long term."

Boeing 747-8F N863GT (c/n 67150), the first 747 built on take-off from Everett-Paine Field on its February 1, 2023, delivery flight. *Boeing*

quotes a maximum revenue payload of 295,000lb (134,000kg) for its 747-8F aircraft.

As well as high capacity, the 747-8F offers operational flexibility, thanks to the multiple loading points: the distinctive upwards-swinging nose cargo door and the main deck side cargo doors on either side of the rear fuselage.

LEAVING THE MARKET

The Boeing 747 symbolised the age of mass air transport, but more efficient engines and extended range operations clearances meant new generations of twin-jet aircraft that entered the market, most notably the Boeing 777-300ER (832 delivered) and the Airbus A350-series (587 delivered), offered comparable range, passenger-carrying capabilities at lower operating costs and revenue-generating underfloor cargo capacity. Such highly capable big twins are now airline flagships.

The result was that the jumbo was overtaken in fulfilling many airlines' high-capacity, long-range needs. This was reflected by the diverging sales fortunes of the 777 and 747 over the long term.

Consequently, on July 29, 2020, Boeing's president and chief executive officer, David Calhoun told staff that the company was to stop building the 747. On January 31, 2023, the company celebrated the delivery of the final aircraft, Boeing 747-8F N863GT, to Atlas Air, ending more than a half century of production.

In a new release, Boeing said: "Boeing employees who designed and built the first

BOEING 747-400 AND 747-8 CHARACTERISTICS		
Characteristic	**747-400**	**747-8**
Wingspan	211ft 5in (64.4m)	224ft 5in (68.4m)
Length	231ft 10in (70.7m)	250ft 2in (76.3m)
Height to top of tail	63ft 8in (19.4m)	63ft 6in (19.3m)
MTOW	[400] 875,000lb (396,894kg) [400ER] 910,000lb (412,770kg) [400F] 875,000lb (396,894kg) [400ERF] 910,000lb (414,130kg)	[8I and 8F] 987,000lb (447,700kg)
Fuel capacity	[400 and 400F] 57,285 US gal (216,824lit) [400ER] 63,460 US gal (240,196lit) [400ERF] 53,985 US gal (204,333lit)	[8I] 63,034 US gal (238,610lit) [8F] 59,734 US gal (226,118lit)
Cruise speed	Mach 0.92	Mach 0.86
Cargo volume	[400] 5,536ft³(156.76m³) [400ER] 4,550ft³(129m³) [400F and 400ERF] Main deck 18,720ft³(530m³) Lower deck 5,536ft³(156.76m³)	[8I] 5,705ft³(161.5m³) [8F] 30,364ft³(859.81m³)
Cargo payload	[400F] 271,046lb (122,945kg) [400ERF] 248,600lb (112,763kg)	[8I] 167,700lb (76,067kg) [8F] 302,400lb (137,160kg)
Engines	CF6-80C2s, PW4056s, PW4200s or RB211-524s	GE Aerospace GEnx-2B

Data: Boeing

747, known as the 'incredibles', returned to be honoured at the Everett factory where the journey of the 747 began in 1967. The factory produced 1,574 airplanes over the life of the

programme. As the first twin-aisle airplane, the 'Queen of the Skies' enabled airlines to connect people across vast distances and provide non-stop trans-oceanic flights. The airplane's core design with its distinctive hump and seating in the upper deck has delighted generations of passengers and operators alike."

When the final aircraft was rolled-out from the Everett factory, in a news release, Boeing announced a couple of interesting facts: "At 250ft 2in in length, the 747-8 is the longest commercial aircraft in service. At typical cruising speeds, the 747-8 travels roughly the length of three FIFA soccer fields or NFL football fields, per second. The final airplane is a 747-8 Freighter. This model has a revenue payload of 133.1 tonnes, enough to transport 10,699 solid-gold bars or approximately 19 million ping-pong balls or golf balls."

The jumbo's ability to fly more than 400 people long haul in one go made it the largest-capacity passenger airliner at the time of its service entry with Pan Am in 1970. The aircraft's 'Queen of the Skies' label, its status as a symbol of American pre-eminence in the aerospace industry, its use as *Air Force One* and above all, its key role in the development of air transport all added to the legend.

People unable to tell a 777 from a 787 or an A330 from an A350 immediately recognise the 747 because of its humpback fuselage, a tall tailfin, or the fact that it has four engines, which in 2024 is a rarity. These days the word iconic is often used to describe many a less-than-iconic machine. The editor doubts the Boeing 787 Dreamliner or the Airbus A350 can ever be called iconic, at least not with any sincerity. But that's not the case with the Boeing 747. When someone refers to the jumbo as iconic, the term is perfectly placed. Most people using the term will not have heard of Joe Sutter, but their choice of terminology serves as recognition to the work that he and his team undertook back in the mid-1960s.

Those readers who are fortunate enough to have flown on a 747 will realise that the aircraft looks good, sounds good and flies good. Nothing turns heads like a 747!

Boeing 747-100 testbed N7470 (c/n 20235), the first 747 built on its roll-out from the Everett Production Factory on September 30, 1968. *Boeing*

Lufthansa's first Boeing 747-8I D-ABYA *Brandenburg* was delivered to the German carrier in April 2012. The jet is seen a moment from touchdown at Los Angeles International Airport. *Chris Wood*

Buccaneers to Jumbos

Facing defence spending cuts while a Buccaneer pilot with the Fleet Air Arm, in the late 1970s Robert Scott applied for Cathay Pacific's pilot training programme. Twenty-three years later he retired as a pilot having flown 12,000 hours on the 747.

Cathay Pacific Boeing 747-467 VR-HUE parked on a stand at Zurich International Airport. Aero Icarus/Wikimedia Commons

Robert Scott started his Boeing 747 training course at King County Airport to the south of Seattle, Washington in 1980. He successfully completed the course and started line training as a first officer with Cathay Pacific Airways, flying from Hong Kong's then Kai Tak Airport.

Recalling his first 747 base training flight, Robert said: "I remember being on approach during circuit training at Kai Tak in this very large aeroplane and looking at the runway and wondering if we were going to be able to stop this thing by the end of the runway. Then of course you get it on the ground, and it stops very quickly because it's so well put together. It's easy to get on the ground because you've got so many wheels underneath you, I've landed the aeroplane in 40kts of crosswind, and it wasn't a problem at all, the aeroplane was very forgiving. It's a

massive aeroplane to taxi and you get used to leading the turn on the corners to make sure you don't overshoot and go off the taxiway."

Providing insight to the work a 747 pilot must complete when taking charge of the aircraft, Robert said: "Preparing and taking over an aeroplane for operation was straightforward. It had to be because so many other people from engineering and catering were involved. On the flight deck we looked at the paperwork, completed the planning which had usually been prepared for you and the routes had been chosen, so we checked what had already been agreed upon, and signed off

on the amount of fuel required based on the en route weather restrictions and the weather on arrival. Occasionally, you may have disagreed with some of the decisions that had already been made so it fell upon you to correct those and make adjustments that you though necessary and agree that with the flight crew.

"Once you'd been through flight planning you went to the aeroplane and followed a standardised procedure to prepare the jet. There weren't many times when you had to make out of the ordinary decisions. One example was the fuel payload based on either or both the weather and the technical state of

> ## "I remember being on approach during circuit training at Kai Tak in this very large aeroplane and looking at the runway and wondering if we were going to be able to stop."

the aeroplane. You referred to the minimum equipment list to help determine whether you could leave with a minor technical problem, which occasionally could incur a fuel penalty. The idea was to set off with the right amount of fuel and that nobody was concerned about encountering a fuel issue on route."

COMETH THE 400

When Robert transitioned to the 400, he was already a training captain, so his transition was somewhat truncated, comprising one four sector trip after which he was training and checking other people on the 400. Describing his training role with the variant, Robert said: "I got an enormous pleasure from teaching people how to use the flight management system because it made life easier given that we'd gone from a three-crew classic to the two-crew 400. Anything that reduced the workload in the cockpit was very welcome.

"In 1998, the company introduced the cadet pilot programme to offer young people the chance to become an airline pilot. This

was a major step forward for Cathay Pacific. Previously, the company had only employed people who were very experienced and never employed anyone with little or no experience at all. I remember doing base training with four second officers one day, and they were cadet pilots. They took to the 400 like ducks to water because the basic training that they'd done in Australia was very good. We made good use of the simulator to prepare them for flying the actual aeroplane in base training. It was amazing to see how well they adapted to flying this huge aeroplane having only ever flown a small twin during their initial training."

Discussing the broader training requirements of Cathay, Robert said: "The company had its requirements for a certain number of training captains and put all of them through a standardisation training programme to ensure that everybody was saying the same thing to the trainee and operating the aeroplane as much as possible to the same standard every time it got airborne. As you gained experience as training captain, as a

position became available, you were moved up to the position of check captain which involved doing check rides with people. In-house training standardised what the new check captains were doing with the pilots.

"Ultimately, if you were considered suitable and a management position became available, then you were invited to join management. Even though there was much less flying involved, it was very enjoyable. It was nice to be in a position where you could make decisions which determined the way the airline was operating, some of which were not operational but commercial in nature.

"Working in a management position I was required to do a minimum number of hours a month though most of us managed to do a bit more than that. At the time I still had my check training qualifications so I could go on training or check rides, which kept me in touch with what was going on. My management work was mainly within the training department, so just about every time I flew, I was checking or training somebody."

A Cathay Pacific Boeing 747-267B landing at Kai Tak with the tower blocks of Kowloon in the background. Konstantin von Wedelstaedt/Wikimedia Commons

Cathay Pacific Boeing 747-400 B-HKF seen on take-off from Hong Kong's former airport at Kai Tak. Konstantin von Wedelstaedt/Wikimedia Commons

> "After about an hour flying the aeroplane, it was as though there'd never been a flight engineer."

During his time working in management, the decision was made to replace the 747 with the 777. This was perceived as being a major step because Cathay Pacific hadn't operated big twins before. However, commenting on the change, Robert said: "It wasn't a major step, it was more of a mental approach to accept that ETOPS was going to be part of the equation in flight planning and required quite a different way of thinking and aeroplane operation. This all led to some interesting discussions because there was an awful lot of concern about twin engine aircraft, but their emergence was accepted by both the airline industry and the travelling public. There is conservatism within the industry, which I think has kept it safe because it's very resistant to change. When Boeing proposed removing the flight engineer on the 747-400 there was huge debate about the proposition. It was of course proven that technology worked, and the aeroplane was just as safe, in fact maybe even safer in many ways, as it was with the three crew."

Robert flew the 747-400 for 14 years, mostly as a training and check captain. There were two main differences between a 747 classic and a 747-400: the 400 featured much more automation, and the flight crew didn't include a flight engineer, so a two-person crew rather than three. By comparison, the classic was fitted with older technology.

Describing the 400, Robert said: "The 400 had a much better navigation system, the automation was better. The autopilot and auto-land systems were very good, as were the auto-throttles, all very well designed. So, from the moment you started the take-off roll you engage the auto-throttle, and that remained engaged for the whole flight, and you engaged the autopilot at a very early stage in the take-off. Having said that, we used to fly manually by a considerable amount just to familiarise the pilots with the feel of the aeroplane. We felt it was a very important for a pilot who is charge of the aircraft to understand how to fly it manually and not to rely totally on the automation."

REFLECTIONS

Describing the 747, Robert said: "It was a delightful aeroplane and amazingly easy to fly considering how large it was. I did three years on the classic before going to the TriStar to do my command training, and then went back to the 747 which by that time was the 400 model. I'd flown the classic and the TriStar with a flight engineer, so I was used to the way things were done in the cockpit and the way the aeroplanes were put together systems wise. So, I was quite curious about what it was going to be like flying the very large 747-400 aeroplane without a flight engineer. Interestingly, after about an hour flying the aeroplane, it was as though there'd never

Cathay Pacific painted Boeing 747-467 B-HOY in a green colour scheme to mark Hong Kong as 'Asia's World City' in 2002. Grahame Hutchison/Wikimedia Commons

been a flight engineer. The aeroplane was so well designed, so well put together, that it was remarkably easy to fly - a shared delight. Within a very short time I was training and checking other people on the 747-400 and then went into different management positions that all involved the 400 model".

Discussing 747 flight operations from Kai Tak, Robert said it was an interesting place to operate in and out of. A reference to its location on the eastern side of Kowloon

Bay and surrounded by mountains, some as close as 1.9 miles away and the infamous chequerboard approach to runway 13. A hill was painted with an orange-white chequerboard as a visual reference on the final approach, a gut-wrenching experience for any passenger with a view of downtown Kowloon a couple of hundred feet below. Commenting on the torrid approach, Robert said: "I always felt a bit of sympathy for people who maybe only flew in and out of Kai

Tak once or twice a year and invariably when the weather was bad, whereas we were doing it just about every day of the week, so it was second nature to us."

As Asian cities go, Hong Kong's location can be considered as 'in the middle of it all'. An ideal location for any airline to operate from. In Robert's early years with Cathay Pacific the carrier flew international routes to other Asian cities. Discussing the routes he flew in those days, he said: "It was a mix.

Boeing 747-400 B-HUI parked on a stand at Hong Kong's Chep Lak Kok Airport. Aero Icarus/Wikimedia Commons

We would do a four-sector day, which would involve flying Kai Tak to Taipei, Taipei to Tokyo, Tokyo back to Taipei and then Taipei back to Kai Tak, which was a busy day. Quite often, we would do long-haul flights such as Sydney. Eventually we went as far as Bahrain and then started flying to Europe, initially to London, and then various other destinations. Once we had 747-400s we flew ultra-long-haul services to Los Angeles and San Francisco. Those routes lasted 14,

15, 16 hours depending on the winds but in terms of weariness were still comfortable to be perfectly honest. There was a period of mental adjustment questioning if it was going to work out, okay, because it was such a change from flying shorter haul. Initially it was difficult to believe this was going to work out well, but you reach a stage when you're completely comfortable flying ultra-long-haul flights, and the accuracy of the information that you're given at departure."

"When the 747 arrived, it wasn't a progressive step but a revolutionary one and made a huge impact on the airline industry. The operating economics of the 747 made it successful from a commercial point of view and it has a remarkable safety record. There has never been a period when the industry and the travelling public were unsure about the 747 and have always remained happy when walking aboard, and it maintains that reputation today with the 747-8. But things change over time, and we now have new types of aeroplanes taking over the 747's place and they are remarkable. My only concern is one that many others have, and that is that we tend to be overwhelmed by technology. There are concerns that there isn't as much time and money put into training pilots these days with a lack of technical knowledge of the aeroplane."

> **"When the 747 arrived, it wasn't a progressive step but a revolutionary one and made a huge impact on the airline industry."**

Three Iconic Aircraft

Richard Gurney learnt to fly on the single piston-engine Piper Cherokee and the twin piston-engine Beechcraft Baron. During his flying career he flew the Handley Page Herald, the BAC 1-11 and ultimately, the 747 with British Airways.

British Airways Boeing 747-436 G-CIVO on final approach to London Heathrow. Chris Wood

British Airways Boeing 747-436 G-CIVU on take-off from London Heathrow. Chris Wood

When Richard Gurney completed his flying training at Hamble in 1981, despite paying for the course, British Airways did not employ him or any of his fellow trainees. At the end of the course, after 150 hours on the Cherokee and 75 hours on the Beechcraft Baron, each trainee received a frozen Airline Transport Pilot Licence (ATPL) instrument and a type rating on the Baron. With no employment prospect with British Airways, Richard got a job with British Air Ferries which provided a type rating course and base training on the Handley Page Herald. He flew revenue-earning services doing oil support in Libya and then passenger services between Tunis and Malta. After two years he left British Air Ferries to join the then Securicor Express flying the company's single Herald on parcel flights between Birmingham and Belfast, Stansted, and Brussels.

Richard then got his first chance to fly a jet-powered aircraft, the BAC 1-11, with Dan Air flying passenger services from Manchester to European holiday destinations. In 1987 during a chance encounter at Gatwick airport with Lynn Barton, the first woman British Airways had trained as a pilot, she told Richard about the then pilot recruitment campaign by British

Airways and encouraged him to apply. Richard took Lynn's advice and after a two-day interview and simulator assessment he received a phone call from a British Airways agent offering him a position and just as surprisingly, asking him what type of aircraft he would like to fly. There was only one, Richard wanted to fly the 747.

Taking up the story, Richard said: "I joined the 747-training programme in August 1987, starting with a three-week induction course at Heathrow followed by the ground school element to learn the technical-, performance- and flying manuals. You went through every single facet of the aeroplane taking progress tests as you progressed. The results formed part of the type rating examination which certified your 747 rating. You used a cockpit procedures trainer to learn instrumentation and practice using the various systems. The instructor entered failures to the system for which the trainee had to use checklists to work their way through non-normal events ordinarily known as emergencies. The follow-on simulator phase comprised 14 sessions which taught you how to fly the 747 without any failures, how to handle the aircraft on take-off, how to fly different types of approach and how to handle a non-normal situation. You practiced dealing with failures in the various systems, how to handle the aircraft in the event of an engine failure both on take-off and at cruise altitude for which you had to perform what's known as a drift down."

A drift down is a maximum thrust/minimum rate descent necessitated by an engine failure in a multi-engine aircraft in the latter stages of climb or during cruise when the aircraft no longer has the power to stay at cruise altitude.

"That got you to the stage of being able to do the type rating test and an instrument rating in the simulator, such that by the time you'd finished your 14 sessions, you were sufficiently qualified to then fly a real aeroplane. At the time, simulators lacked the fidelity to emulate the aircraft closely enough, so you had to do base training. That involved a training captain and a training first officer flying a 747-100 from Heathrow to Shannon airport Ireland with ten trainees onboard. Each trainee flew four circuits with touch and go landings or go arounds flown on each circuit with one full-stop landing to enable the trainee to swap for the next one. This phase enabled you to handle the real aircraft in a non-revenue environment.

"The next stage was route training which comprised 26 sectors flown with a training captain in a real aeroplane with passengers onboard. My first ever trip lasted 12 days involving Heathrow to Bombay in a 200 series, a flight down to Colombo in Sri Lanka and return. Then we flew as passengers to Dubai from where we flew a 747 to Hong Kong. We then flew a shuttle service to Beijing and back in a day followed by Hong Kong to Delhi

> *"In those days, the 100-series aircraft lacked the range to reach Tokyo in one hop. We flew from Heathrow to Anchorage, stayed there for two nights, then flew to Tokyo."*

Captain Richard Gurney in the left seat and his colleague, first officer Mike Perks on the flight deck of a Boeing 747-436. *British Airways/Richard Gurney*

and then Delhi to Heathrow. We flew each leg, except for the Beijing shuttle, with a statutory rest period, with a two-night rest at Bombay because in those days there were only four services from London per week, so we had to wait for the next aircraft to arrive.

"A service to Tokyo routed via Anchorage, Alaska because of Soviet restrictions on the use of its airspace, and in those days, the 100-series aircraft lacked the range to reach

A British Airways Boeing 747-400 on a parking spot at London Heathrow. *British Airways/Richard Gurney*

Tokyo in one hop. We flew from Heathrow to Anchorage, stayed there for two nights, then flew to Tokyo and then down to Osaka. We then returned along the same line via Tokyo, Anchorage and back to London. A nine-day trip. Toward the end of your route training, you were recommended for your final route check, mine was to New York-JFK. Upon successful completion of that trip, you were cleared out on the line as a qualified co-pilot (first officer)."

A British Airways Boeing 747-400 high over the north Atlantic. British Airways/Richard Gurney

ROUTE TRAINING

Richard's first real route training trip was again from Heathrow to Bombay. The entire day was different to anything he'd done before in terms of the length of the flight, where he was heading and the duration of the trip. Recalling the day, Richard said: "During the brief a serious man working behind the desk handed you a print-out of the flight plan and then briefed us, which was intriguing. The captain then made his fuel decision and then asked me if I had a considered opinion on the fuel? Of course, I didn't have any opinions because I didn't know what the 747 traits were with respect to the flight plan and en route weather. The fuel was ordered, the aircraft's technical status was reviewed, and we went out to the aeroplane on the crew bus. At the bottom of the stairs, looking up I remember thinking how big the aircraft is and how will it get airborne?

"Once on the flight deck, I remember the speed that things happened. It took 70 minutes until we pushed back and there was a lot to do in that time. The crew comprised the captain, a safety co-pilot, me as first officer, and two flight engineers, one of whom was in training. While the safety co-pilot completed the walkaround, I reviewed the technical log, which is the write up of the state of the aeroplane, with the flight engineer. Having established what was wrong with the aeroplane, if anything, we used the manual called the minimum equipment list to review whether there were special procedures that had to be followed. I then went through the pre-flight checks on my side of the cockpit.

"Because a 747 classic lacked sufficient memory in its flight management system, you had to load all the waypoints manually, so loading a nine-hour route to Bombay was quite a time-consuming process because I wasn't familiar with any of the places outside of Europe. Then you had to do a briefing for the captain and the flight engineers about what was going to happen and what you were

> **"The best remedy was to depower everything, take the ground power off and drop the APU and then turn the battery off. Leave it for 30 seconds, put the battery back on again."**

going to do in the event of an emergency. One of the joys about the 747 classic was having a flight engineer as part of the crew who did a huge amount of the pre-flight preparation. At the time of push back, as first officer I was not involved with starting the engines because that was something that the captain and the flight engineer did.

"Once at the end of the runway, during the take-off run, the 200 series aircraft with Rolls-Royce engines seemed so powerful. We took off on a westerly runway at Heathrow and I remember the aircraft accelerating so quickly and the captain advising me to pull the nose up more to limit the accelerating energy and avoid exceeding the flap limiting speed [flaps, slats and landing gears have limiting speeds to avoid over stressing them]. If you haven't got the nose up in the air, more of the energy accelerates the aircraft rather than helping it climb. Close to the flap limiting speed, I got it under control after which it became more manageable, which was a big learning point.

"When flying over Saudi Arabia, the captain turned to me and said it was my turn to have a break. What do you mean I replied? You can have a lie down now; we'll give you a shout when it's the next person's turn to have a rest. I didn't want to have a rest because it was my first time flying in this part of the world, so I stayed on the flight deck and the safety-first officer went back to bed. To me it was extraordinary to see that part of the world for the first time. You had to do the first six landings on your route training to get used to handling the aeroplane, for me that meant landing at Bombay Airport which has quite a challenging approach and doesn't have the longest of runways.

"Bombay's instrument landing system had a 3.3° glidepath, so a little steeper than most airports, which required you to fly a slightly higher rate of descent to avoid local terrain. You land the 747 with either 25 or 30° of flap. You had to use 30° of flap at Bombay and because the runway was 9,760ft long you really didn't want to flare the aircraft and carry on down the runway before landing because that wastes a lot of the runway's length. At Bombay you had to use full reverse thrust. My landing was firm but OK, and we cleared the runway where we were supposed to exit, but the thing I remember most was the smell entering the aircraft through the pressurisation system outflow valves that open after landing."

Richard flew his last 747 classic on October 16, 1990, and his first 747-400 flight on December 10. Because he had lots of experience as a 747 pilot, his transition course for the 400 was truncated. Giving a brief synopsis of the 400 course, Richard said: "Ground school was 12 days, most of which was dedicated to learning about the automation and the screens [the electronic flight information system dubbed EFIS] which introduced a different way of operating the aircraft. A simulator phase followed, comprising eight simulator sessions and then an instrument rating test, but no base training because the simulators had the fidelity to properly emulate the aircraft, and then you did route training. This involved six sectors including a two-sector route

A rainy roll-out after landing at London Heathrow for this Boeing 747-400. British Airways/Richard Gurney

Cargo on the stand awaits loading on board a Boeing 747-400. British Airways/Richard Gurney

> "Lord King, the then chairman of British Airways, was a passenger on a flight from Los Angeles to Heathrow with me as the co-pilot. Our departure was delayed because of an advisory message."

check with a training captain after which we went out to fly the line, mostly routes familiar to me.

"Every now and then when you were powering up the 400's systems, the thing would get in a muddle [not when it was powered up] and system error messages were displayed on the EFIS screens, but you wouldn't be able to make it go away. The best remedy was to depower everything, take the ground power off and drop the APU and then turn the battery off. Leave it for 30 seconds, put the battery back on again, then bring AC power onto the aeroplane and then work through setting up the various systems. Invariably the problem went away because the string of computers got in a bit of a muddle.

"The 400 displayed messages on the upper EFIS screen comprising cautions, advisories and master warnings displayed in priority order with audio sound telling you what it wanted you to do next. The 400 was also equipped with an early version of control automation with a computer controlling an artificial feel force exerted by an actuator to the control column to simulate changes in both airspeed and flight control forces."

LORD KING
Explaining the artificial feel force, Richard said: "It felt like you were controlling the flight controls on the wings or the rudder by a direct linkage system to the control surfaces although there was no physical linkage involved, all your control inputs were through cables to hydraulic actuators adjacent to the flight control surfaces. The autopilot inputs went directly to the hydraulic servos. The aircraft was very good at making you feel part of it.

"Lord King, the then chairman of British Airways, was a passenger on a flight from Los Angeles to Heathrow with me as the co-pilot. Our departure was delayed because of an advisory message shown on the upper EFIS screen. The engineers couldn't rectify the fault, so I suggested switching the aircraft off and starting again for a re-boot. That got rejected by the engineers. Lord King came up on the flight deck and asked why we were delayed. While King was on the flight deck, I once again suggested we just switch it off and turn it back on. 'We know it works sometimes', I said. The engineer once again rejected the idea. Lord King touched the engineer's arm and said, 'why don't you do what the young man says?'. After advising the passengers what we were doing, we depowered the aeroplane, and after 30 seconds, turned it on, the system re-booted and without the fault, which allowed us to go back to London."

Richard liked flying the 747, not least the 400 which offered one stand-out flight deck environment advantage. Explaining, he said: "The classic had two upper deck doors just behind the flight deck entrance door which was always a bit noisy. On the 400, the upper deck doors were halfway back and properly insulated. Consequently a 400 was so much quieter than a classic and a joy to operate."

During his time serving with British Airways, Richard flew 747 classic and 400 series as a first officer, then the Boeing 777 as captain for three years before a return to the 747-400 for a 12-year stint as a captain. His career then took him back to the 777 as a captain before retiring in 2018.

Flying Jumbos in the Orient

Nigel Hughes served as a Boeing 747 pilot with Cathay Pacific Airways for many years and recalls some of his memories of flying the jumbo.

Cathay Pacific Cargo Boeing 747-867F B-LJI on take-off from Ted Stevens Anchorage International Airport. Chris Wood

Nigel Hughes first flew the Boeing 747 with British Airways in 1987. As a child he lived near Shannon Airport in Ireland and remembers watching the first 747 land there at the start of a European tour. As part of his base training, he was the first pilot to fly a BA 747 into the Irish super hub.

Nigel spent just a year at BA flying the 747-100 and 747-200 models before joining Cathay Pacific where his flying career included all the carrier's widebody types. Initially he flew the 747-200 and 747-300 from Kai Tak Airport, the long-time home of Cathay, transitioned to the 747-400, followed by the L-1011 TriStar on which he gained his command credentials, then transitioned to the Airbus A330, returned to the 747-400, then the original 747-8, and finally the 777-300.

But that's not the complete story, as Nigel explained: "During the COVID pandemic, Cathay was looking for volunteers to fly cargo, so I went back to the 747, this time the 747-400ER freighters, and then back to the 747-8,

this time the freighter, which by then was a joy to fly compared to the aircraft in its original configuration.

"During my career, I completed five 747 transition courses. I had lost my rating on the aircraft each time and had to do a full conversion course, comprising ground school, simulator sessions, and some airborne training. When I came off the 777, I had a slightly truncated course because it was a Boeing-to-Boeing ethos. The others were from Airbus or TriStar and were full course programmes.

"My notes from my first 400 transition course are much more comprehensive when compared with the second 400 transition 20 years later. Back then they taught us more about the aircraft and then cut costs on the training, so pilots had far less system knowledge than those trained 20 years ago.

"My transition from the classic to the 400 was probably the toughest because the aeroplane was brand new, so all the instructors were learning the EFIS system. For the 400 freighter I had a one-day course. When I first flew the original passenger and freighter variants, I was qualified on eight different types of 747 counting each model and the engine type combinations."

Describing the 747, Nigel said: "It's a beautifully designed aircraft and was just a dream to fly. She was so balanced in turbulence and when landing in cross winds, she was just a gem. The 200 and the 100 handled the same, the 200 held more fuel and had more powerful engines, but you wouldn't really notice the difference. The 300 had an extended upper deck."

Nigel was a first officer with Cathay when the carrier introduced the 400. He recalled: "It was the first aircraft operated by Cathay equipped with an electronic flight instrument system [EFIS] in the cockpit. Our pilots had to transition from the analogue cockpit to EFIS which really challenged the senior captains because of the sheer amount of information on the displays such that they couldn't filter out what was important and what was not.

"On the classics, the MCP [mode control panel] was just below the window where you could dial in the ILS or VOR frequency. With EFIS you had to go into the screen menu and to type it in to the computer. So, flying a VOR DME on the EFIS into, for example Frankfurt Airport, was much more complex than on the classic's analogue MCP, so the senior captains tended to fall behind the aircraft and lost situational awareness.

"Designed for long haul routes, the 400's primary difference to the classics was EFIS and even though the 400 had more power, take-off weights were generally heavier, so the pilot didn't notice it dynamically because the power to weight ratio was probably the same as the 100. The only time pilots noticed the extra power was during a go around with low fuel."

Nigel described the initial 747-8, Boeing's final model of the jumbo, as "a real missed opportunity for Boeing."

He continued: "When Boeing was designing the 8, they wanted it to have the same type rating as the 400. To achieve that, they couldn't have more than 30% of the cockpit different to the 400 so they dumbed it down to make it look like a 400 cockpit. Whereas they could have made a technology jump to make the cockpit more sophisticated than the 777's at the time. Consequently, when flying the 8 you were always flying an aircraft that had more potential than it had, with lots of growing pain issues that they really should not have had. It has a considerably different and beautiful wing with very powerful General Electric GEnx engines, so it should have been a beauty from day one, but it wasn't. I didn't like it because things didn't work and preferred flying the 400ERF freighter. The 400ERFs were the sweetest 747s ever built. Several

> ## "When I first flew the original passenger and freighter variants, I was qualified on eight different types of 747 counting each model and the engine type combinations."

years later when I went back onto the 8, the growing pain issues had been solved and in some ways the technology was ahead of the 777-300ER, for example, you could fly quite sophisticated GPS approaches. By then the 8 was also a beauty."

Discussing the difference between flying passenger services to cargo, Nigel said: "I preferred passenger because we always had a bus waiting for us, and the infrastructure at the airport of arrival was always slicker, in cargo we had to sort ourselves out. When I went back to flying cargo on the 8F during the COVID pandemic, the upper deck was the crew area fitted with six business class seats and two cabins. We could prepare our own food and coffee, A culture had developed where everybody helped each other make the meals so it turned into a little flying club, and I ended up loving cargo flying more

than passenger flights. With no passengers, nobody arrived at the aeroplane late and nobody got drunk, so it was a very stress free, easy operation."

During his career at Cathay, the main airport at Hong Kong moved from Kai Tak to the man-made island dubbed Chek Lap Kok. Its location is between two the mountains on Lantau Island to the south and those to the north on mainland China. The mountains cause what's known as rotary turbulence which makes it more perilous to land than the intricacies of landing at Kai Tak as Nigel explained: "The ILS gets interfered with by the mountain, so air traffic control gives you GPS approaches when you really want an ILS for weather. In general air traffic control provided workarounds for all the little issues they have there. I preferred the hustle and bustle of Kai Tak, because we got very

Cathay Pacific Cargo Boeing 747-467ERF B-LIC at Amsterdam-Schiphol Airport, the Netherlands. Alf van Beem/Wikimedia Commons

Cathay Pacific Airways Boeing 747-467 B-HOS landing at Chep Lak Kok Airport, Hong Kong. *Konstantin von Wedelstaedt/Wikimedia Commons*

"With no passengers, nobody arrived at the aeroplane late and nobody got drunk, so it was a very stress free, easy operation."

good at the curved approaches, and I don't remember weather related issues at Kai Tak being anywhere near what we experienced at Chek Lap Kok.

"At Cathay, the general rule was that a cargo flight would be six to nine hours, you'd land, the crew changed, you had a day off and then continue down route. We flew to the Middle East and then to Europe or to India and then to Europe. We flew to Alaska, stay there for a day or two, and then fly around the US and Mexico. If the load was light, you could fly an ultra-long haul or if you were ferrying an aircraft, you would fly New York to Hong Kong direct. But with a full heavy load, your flight was shorter than an average passenger flight unless you were in a part of the world where they play fast and loose on the load sheets. If you had a very heavy load and wanted to make sure it's strapped down because you're not happy, you'd get the loading supervisor out, and go through the books to ensure everything is loaded correctly. I once kicked a 37-tonne piece of equipment off, because they couldn't satisfy me that they had loaded it properly. I was called by my fleet manager who asked why I had done that, I explained, and he agreed. Cathay always backed my decisions."

Summing up, Nigel said: "The 747 is built like a brick house. If you made a heavy landing in an Airbus 340-600, you had to change the undercarriage, but in a Boeing 747 you'd never have to change anything. She was beautifully designed, didn't have dynamic stability so you had to fly it where you wanted it to go but you didn't have to put a lot of control stick input in, to get it to do what you wanted. She was very easy to fly, her controllability was just fantastic as was her responsiveness, she was a highly balanced and well-designed aircraft."

Helicopters, Turboprops and 747s

Chris Wood had a varied career before he piloted a Boeing 747. Having served with the Fleet Air Arm piloting military types, he flew a variety of civil aircraft with Dan Air before joining Virgin Atlantic to fly the 747-200.

When Chris Wood joined Virgin Atlantic, the company was growing and hiring lots of pilots after its owner, Richard Branson, won the quite famous dirty tricks case against British Airways. Chris followed the standard training programme, which started with three weeks of technical ground school learning the aircraft systems, taught by highly experienced and knowledgeable flight engineers. This was followed by a week's ancillary classroom training for subjects such as weight and balance and safety equipment and procedures [SEP]. Next was the simulator phase which involved ten mammoth four-hour sessions learning how to fly and operate the aircraft, and deal with malfunctions. This was followed by the most exciting bit, base training. This was usually done at a quiet regional, or occasionally military, airport; in Chris' case Chateauroux in France was used. This was his first chance to actually fly a 747. Explaining the day's activity, Chris said: "We were just flying circuits like you would do in a Cessna, or any other aircraft, which seemed quite surreal in such a large aircraft. We had to do a minimum of five landings each, after the fifth we flew a wide circuit to enable the student pilot to swap for the next guy. If we'd landed for each changeover brake heating could've been an issue. You didn't get that much of a feel for flying the aircraft doing circuits, but the touch and goes, and the landing were mandatory requirements. Compared to anything else we'd flown, the flight deck was much higher off the ground which took a bit a bit of getting used to and made for an interesting landing. You had to flare much sooner, but you were helped by the flight engineer counting the height down.

"The 747 burns around 12 tonnes of fuel an hour [0.2 tonnes per minute] so in terms of saving fuel and money, every minute counts."

All of Virgin Atlantic's Boeing 747s were given names, G-VBIG was called Tinker Bell. *Chris Wood*

He'd read the height off the radio altimeter for the last 50 feet, calling 50, 40, 30, 20, 10 feet. At around 30 feet you started the flare easing the power off to idle, to ideally achieve a smooth touchdown at the aiming point on the runway 1,500 feet from the threshold. Occasionally the flight engineer's count down was faster due to the rate of descent, so unless you started the flare a little earlier, you could expect a firm arrival carrier style! If the countdown was slower, you knew you had flared too soon and were at risk of floating down the runway, increasing the risk of a tailstrike."

For a reader unfamiliar with the term flare, this is a manoeuvre conducted during the landing of an aircraft, when the control column is eased back to raise the nose of the aircraft to reduce the descent rate to achieve a smooth touchdown.

ROUTE TRAINING

Chris successfully completed base training and then went to the Civil Aviation Authority

Hot Lips, *the name given to Virgin Atlantic Airways Boeing 747-443 G-VLIP seen at Las Vegas McCarran International Airport on March 25, 2016. Chris Wood*

> "Occasionally the flight engineer's count down was faster due to the rate of descent, so you expected the jet to thump down on the runway."

to add the 747 type rating to his licence. This cleared the way for the last part of training, known as line training. This saw him flying on operational flights as a first officer under the supervision of a training captain. His first flight was the VS9 to New York, JFK. Discussing route training he said: "We always shared the flying based on the sectors involved. For a normal two-sector trip generally one pilot flies out and the other flies back. There are various factors that influence the decision, weather is one and suitability of the airport is another, there are a few airports that require the captain to do the landing. The decision was usually made on the day after studying the flight paperwork. For his inaugural trip, the captain flew the outbound sector and Chris flew the overnight return to Heathrow."

Chris's training captain was a former British Airways pilot who had flown 747s since the type's very early days, so he had a wealth of knowledge and experience. Recalling the flight Chris said: "The elements that were new for me were the oceanic procedures, how to obtain a clearance to enter the oceanic airspace, and how and when to make position reports. Back then it was all done by voice and radio, now it's all done by datalink.

"The route for every flight is planned by a dedicated flight planner, who uses a computer fed with weather and air traffic data to calculate the optimal route. This is generally achieved by finding the shortest flight time, although overflight charges also come in to play. The jet stream normally blows west to east, so you try to avoid the jet stream going west, and when flying east, you try to get into the jet stream to get the most tailwind to get back quicker. The 747-200 burns around 12 tonnes of fuel an hour [0.2 tonnes per minute] so in terms of saving fuel and money, every minute counts."

Chris also recalled the set-up procedures: "Each pilot had their own area of responsibility requiring you to go around and check that all the switches were in the right place for start-up. A critical part of the set-up procedures was calculating the take-off performance, and working out the required power setting and speeds. This was normally done by the first officer and independently verified by the flight engineer and the captain.

"Another critical part of the set up procedures was programming the navigation system. Modern aeroplanes have flight management computers [FMCs], but in the case of the 747-200, the aircraft had three independent Litton 72 inertial navigation systems [INS] which would only accept nine waypoints.

"As part of the set-up process, the route was loaded into the INS. Normally the pilot flying the sector would do this and once the data had been loaded into one, you would transfer the data to the other two. Then the other pilot

Hot Lips *again, this time seen at London-Gatwick on June 12, 2008. Chris Wood*

A crowded photo showing Virgin Atlantic Airways Boeing 747-443 G-VROY Pretty Woman, *Sun Country Boeing 737-8Q8 N804SY, and the Las Vegas McCarran Airport control tower. Chris Wood*

Virgin Atlantic's first Jumbo, Boeing 747-287B G-VIRG Maiden Voyager seen at Chateauroux Airport, France during crew training, June 17, 1993. Chris Wood

and the flight engineer would independently confirm the data was correct by checking the coordinates and tracks and distances between waypoints. It was very important to get this right, hence the independent checking. An error could see the aircraft departing from its cleared route, which was not desirable. To maintain the integrity of the INS position, the three systems could communicate with each other and would establish an average position. If one of them started to develop an error and wander off, the other two systems would detect this and ignore it.

"The 747-400 had triple inertial reference system [IRS] and flight management computers [FMCs] with the capability to store thousands of waypoints which made it possible to download the route directly into

the FMCs by datalink. However the data still needed to be thoroughly checked for errors.

"When we flew 747-200s to Tokyo, you'd spend a large part of the 12 to 13-hour flight constantly updating the waypoints to prevent the aircraft getting to the last one and deviating from the cleared route. An upgrade to the Litton 92 with a 100-waypoint capacity made life a lot easier!

"When under radar coverage there was generally no requirement for position reports, but over remote areas there was, with reports being made by HF radio. A position report was made for every waypoint to the controlling authority, for the North Atlantic there are five, Shanwick [a combination of Shannon and Prestwick] for the northeast sector, Gander for the northwest sector, Iceland for the north,

> "When we flew 747 classics to Tokyo, you'd spend a large part of the 12 to 13-hour flight constantly updating the waypoints to prevent the aircraft from deviating."

Virgin Atlantic Airways Boeing 747-41R G-VAST Ladybird on climb-out from Las Vegas McCarran International Airport. Chris Wood

Virgin Atlantic Airways
Boeing 747-443 G-VROY
Pretty Woman *high over
the North Atlantic on April
15, 2011. Chris Wood*

Another photo of Boeing 747-287B G-VIRG Maiden Voyager at Chateauroux Airport. Chris Wood

Santa Maria in the Azores for the southeast sector and New York for the southwest sector. Reports were made in a designated format, but the frequency could be shared with many other aircraft all trying to make position reports and sometimes you could wait almost the whole time between two waypoints to get your call in.

"Today, it's all done automatically. Approaching the ocean, you log on to controller–pilot data link communications [CPDLC] and the aeroplane automatically reports its position. Very occasionally there's a glitch and the controlling authority will ask

for a report by voice communication because they haven't received an automated one, but generally the system works well. You can also use CPDLC to request a climb, a descent, a re-route, weather or a diversion on the odd occasion that's required. Overland the CPDLC works through VHF radio and over an ocean or a remote area through satellite or SATCOM.

"As you come off the ocean, you're given an initial frequency to contact the domestic controlling authority [nowadays through CPDLC]; Gander or New York on the west side of the Atlantic; either Shannon, or Scottish or Brest in France on the east side. Once the air

traffic agency sees you on their radar, they normally give you a direct routing to the flight information region [FIR] boundary, or the start of the arrival procedure for your destination. On Christmas Day you might even get direct to the outer marker for Heathrow or Gatwick."

Chris recalled flying to Los Angeles for the first time: "Approaching from the north over Santa Monica on a beautiful summer's day, it didn't appear to be busy so I asked the training captain if I could get a visual approach. He asked air traffic control and they said yes. The arrival route took us in to a downwind position setting us up nicely. So, I made a visual approach into LAX in

> "The 400 was designed to be flown by a two-pilot crew, although for long flights extra pilots could be carried."

Virgin Atlantic Airways Boeing 747-443 G-VROY Pretty Woman *trailing over the North Atlantic on April 15, 2011. Chris Wood*

a 747, a pinch yourself moment! I was reminded again how easy the aircraft is to fly. With a press of two buttons to disengage the autopilot and the auto-throttle, it turns like it's a big Cessna.

"During line training you fly a prescribed number of sectors with a training captain. Assuming it all goes well, you progress to a check flight known as a line check and if successful you are released from training and cleared to fly with any other company pilot."

DIVERTING A 747

The vast majority of flights proceed without any problems. However very occasionally an

incident will necessitate a diversion. The 747 is very reliable and has a lot of redundancy so most diversions are for problems with people rather than the aeroplane. There are a whole series of procedures that need to be followed by both the cabin crew and the flight deck crew when someone falls ill onboard as Chris explained: "The first thing to do is assess how ill the passenger is and to aid this the company uses a medical services provider, in my time it was one based in Phoenix Arizona. We also carry diagnostic kit onboard which can datalink information to the medical services provider, aiding diagnosis. Their

medical staff are aware of the implications of being airborne and having made a diagnosis can advise the most appropriate course of action, in consultation with the company's operations department.

"If the patient's condition is serious enough to warrant a diversion the aircraft must be prepared for an approach and landing at the diversion airport. This will involve co-ordination with air traffic control and re-programming of the navigation system. Meanwhile the cabin crew will be preparing the cabin for arrival at the diversion airport. The company's operations department will

Ladybird, *Virgin Atlantic Airways Boeing 747-41R G-VAST at Las Vegas McCarran Nevada in August 2009.* Chris Wood

be in contact with the airport to arrange assistance, for example for fuel.

"Fuel load is another consideration. If the aircraft is above the maximum landing weight fuel dumping may be required, although an overweight landing is a consideration if the patient's condition is critical. If under radar control the air traffic control agency will endeavour to provide direct routing to the diversion airfield. The company's operations department also knows of the situation and will liaise with the diversion airport, so the ground services are expecting you.

"On arrival at the stand, the first consideration is to offload the sick passenger, keep the other passengers informed and make the arrangements for getting underway again. This will invariably involve refuelling the aircraft, getting a route from flight planning, reprogramming the navigation system, conducting all pre-flight procedures, and signing off the technical log if there is not a qualified engineer at the location. That all eats into the allowable duty hours and one factor that determines how long your planned duty hours can be is the number of sectors flown. Each sector reduces the allowable duty period."

TRANSITION TO THE BOEING 747-400

Chris flew the 747-200 for a number of years and then the opportunity arose to transition to the 747-400 as the company's fleet grew. This saw him back in the classroom for the training course, although by now it was mostly done by computer as Chris explained: "The transition course was similar to the one for the 747-200, but with eight simulator sessions. The 400's simulator was a high-fidelity system and closely emulated a real aeroplane. This allowed some of the flying training to be transferred to the simulator, and there was no requirement for base training in the aircraft. This not only saved the company money, it also avoided the disruption caused by having to generate an aircraft for a non-revenue flight."

Consequently, the first time Chris flew a 747-400, there were hundreds of passengers onboard, which today is standard for most types of airliner.

Recalling the differences with flying the 400 compared to a 200, Chris explained: "You had to learn how to manage and prioritise information provided to the pilots, with a glass cockpit there was a vast amount. The second

thing was not having a flight engineer, the 400 was designed to be flown by a two-pilot crew, although for long flights extra pilots could be carried.

"Whilst fundamentally the same aircraft, the 400's systems were updated and the automation was much better, particularly the autopilot. The aircraft was designed to be flown by the autopilot [one of three] which reduced the workload significantly, almost a reverse of the classic versions, where it could struggle and the tendency was to disengage the autopilot and fly manually. The auto-throttle on the early classics only worked below 250kts, it was an approach auto-throttle and therefore required the pilots and the flight engineer to monitor and adjust the power accordingly to maintain the required cruising speed whereas the later classics and the 400 had a much better auto-throttle."

Powered by four latest-generation engines, the options were Pratt & Whitney 4000s, General Electric CF6-80C2s or Rolls-Royce RB211-524s, generating more thrust, additional power that was only ever noticeable to the pilot when the aeroplane was empty. Chris said: "Despite using reduced power

"*The 400 has a maintenance computer which is one of the first things the engineers looked at to see what faults had been thrown up, many of which were momentary things that cleared when reset.*"

for take-off, an empty 400 went up like a homesick angel. With classics, it depended to some degree on the type of engine you were using. There were various fits: the more advanced the engine type, the more power. Both the classic and the 400 were easier to fly when heavy because the climb rate wasn't so high, but they were much livelier when empty. At maximum take-off weight, a 400 would be close to 400 tons, empty it was around 200 tons, with up to 240,000lb of thrust."

TAKING CHARGE
When a new flight deck crew arrived at a 747-400 on the stand for the flight ahead, the aircraft should have been through its turnaround. From a maintenance perspective, the engineers had a checklist of things to do which started with checking the engine oil levels within half an hour of shutdown from the previous flight. The 400 had a maintenance computer which was one of the first things the engineers looked at to see what faults had been thrown up, many of which were momentary things that cleared when reset. The aeroplane's tyres would have been checked and changed if necessary: a good team could change a 747 wheel in 45 minutes,

and most destinations had spare wheels on hand.

If there were any defects that couldn't be rectified immediately there was a manual called the minimum equipment list [MEL] which was consulted by the pilots and engineers to see if the defect was acceptable for flight. The MEL would clarify this and laid down any required maintenance actions to be completed prior to despatch. Providing an example, Chris said: "You could go with one electrical generator inoperative because the electrical load is transferred to the operative generators [one advantage of having four!] provided the unserviceable generator had been disconnected.

"But you couldn't go with one hydraulic system inoperative, even though you had four, they must all be working. Each hydraulic system has two pumps, an engine driven pump and a back-up pump. Despatch can be

made with one back up pump inoperative. If the inoperative pump was on systems one or four it was more significant because these systems power the landing gear retraction. In the highly unlikely event of the engine driven pump or engine failing for the associated system and consequent loss of that hydraulic system between passing the V1 speed and the gear being fully retracted, the gear would not retract. Therefore you had to calculate your take-off performance assuming the gear stayed down. This is all outlined in the MEL."

Concluding, Chris said: "The 747 was a marvellous feat of engineering, a lovely aeroplane to fly and loved by everyone involved with it. It was very well designed, had loads of redundancy for all the systems; belt, braces, safety pin and elastic band, and rarely went wrong. It seems such a shame that they are mostly gone from the skies now."

Virgin Atlantic Airways' Boeing 747-443 G-VLIP Hot Lips at Orlando International Airport, Florida. *Chris Wood*

Phantoms, Tornados and Jumbos

After a career with the Royal Air Force flying F-4 Phantoms and Tornado F3s, in 1999 Peter Legg got a job with Virgin Atlantic to continue his flying career, this time on the 747.

Peter Legg sought the advice of some pilot friends about how he might get a pilot job with Virgin Atlantic. Their advice was to apply for the company's crew resource management course comprising an interview and a simulator assessment. According to Peter: "The process was as much about my aptitude to fly the 747 as it was about my ability to fit in to a crew environment. Clearly, I did and that was it."

JUMBO TRAINING

Once selected, Peter completed the company's 747-training course which comprised the standard ground school led by flight engineer instructor Mike Simpson. Peter rated Mike very highly: "Mike had probably forgotten more about the 747 than I ever knew. You had fixed-base simulator sessions. So, for example, after lessons on the fuel system we used the fixed base simulator to operate the fuel system to see how it works. This process was repeated for all the 747's major systems such as hydraulics and flight controls and was designed to gradually build up your knowledge of the aircraft.

"You then moved on to the flight simulator phase comprising 12 four-hour sessions run by instructors and flight engineers from the company's training flight. In my entire flying career, I only ever failed two simulator sessions. One was simulator six on the 747 course when doing a go around. This is a serious event with a list of procedures that must be completed. After the session was complete, my instructor said: "Peter, you haven't understood that. You don't get it. 'No', I replied. Right, he said, we'll do it again. He gave me a good briefing and told me to think of it as a cassette. When it suddenly says, go around, you run through the drill procedure. He was right. In the next session, it went well. My first attempt went wrong because I was used to the military procedures and not this one.

"Simulator ten was known as the line proficiency check which determines if you are fully capable to operate as a first officer on the 747-200 classic as it was then. Simulator ten also included your instrument rating. Simulator 11 introduced you to low visibility operations, in those days referred to as Cat 1, Cat 2 and Cat 3 ops and simulator 12 was called pre-base training, a three-hour sim session dedicated to practicing flying circuits.

"Because you'd never flown anything of substantial size before, you couldn't go straight from the simulator to line flying with passengers. You had to complete base training which involved one take-off for four touch and goes and the final landing, overseen by qualified line trainers. My base training was flown at Prestwick and lasted 40 minutes.

"After five brand new first officers had thumped the 747 aircraft onto the runway at various points, the instructors scored how effective each of us were based on their observations of our performance. Jokingly they also scored our effectiveness by the amount of 'rubber jungle', a colloquial term for the emergency oxygen masks, that had been dislodged in the back of the aircraft. How hard you landed was judged on how many of the oxygen masks you dislodged. Between us we had five rows down at the back end.

"Once base training was successfully completed, you're off and running for line training for which we flew commercial flights with a line training captain and passengers. At the time, I had to fly 18 sectors, then my line release check which is your last training flight with a line trainer. You then fly one more trip with a captain but observed by a training captain, and if successful you're signed off ready to go, and that's the end of your training.

"For my 13th trip, I flew to Miami, and remember in those days, we had flight engineers on the classic, mine was a former British Airways officer and very experienced. I'm flying down the approach, and through my own fault, got too close to the aircraft in front of us. Air traffic cleared us for a go around, remember my instructor had taught me how to do it properly, and during the downwind leg the training instructor pilot, Tim Butler, recommended that if air traffic turns you in a bit tight, look at the TCAS display, and you can adjust your turn to get a greater separation to other arriving traffic. Air traffic asked us to turn in, we had beautiful separation, then on final approach the aircraft in front burst a tyre on landing blocking the runway. So, air traffic tells us to go around again for another approach and this time we landed. As we're taxiing to the terminal, the flight engineer leans forward and said 'Leggy, thank you very bloody much for that'. I asked what was wrong? 'I've been flying for 40 years, and you've just doubled the number of go arounds I've got. Apart from that, the rest of the training was uneventful. Then you start line flying."

Peter recalled his duty on the day of the 9/11 terror attacks: "On September 11, 2001, I was due to fly to Toronto. We pushed off the stand and taxied out and were good to go. Air traffic called to advise there was some sort of security incident going on and we needed to return to the stand. We taxied back with very little information, nobody knew what was going on, so we sat there for a while. Then the captain went on to the PA and said 'Ladies and gentlemen, boys, and girls. we're terribly sorry, there has been some sort of security incident in the United States which were not 100% sure

> "How hard you landed was judged on how many of the oxygen masks you dislodged. Between us we had five rows down at the back end."

Virgin Atlantic Airways' Boeing 747-443 G-VGAL Jersey Girl at Belfast International Airport. Chris Wood

about, so we'll do what we British always do at times like this, have a cup of tea'. So, we had tea and were then told nobody was going anywhere that day, sadly. After 9/11, lots of Virgin flight crew got made redundant including myself, so I decided to re-join the RAF and served until 2004 when I re-joined Virgin on the 747-400."

ONBOARD INCIDENTS

Providing some insight of how a regular line flight can be affected by an incident, Peter gave some examples: "Flying back from Orlando to Manchester with captain Tim Hill there was a disruptive passenger on board and the cabin crew weren't confident they could handle him. So, we diverted to Gander in Newfoundland, where we offloaded the gentleman, left him there, and continued to Manchester. It turned out he was travelling with his family who were in the upper-class cabin and were more than pleased to get rid of him.

"On another occasion I was flying from Orlando to Gatwick, it was a flight in the days before Virgin used MedLink who provide medical emergency services to crews when airborne. We had a woman onboard who was not well, so we diverted to Gander. Given the time spent managing the emergency while on the ground at Gander, we ran out of duty hours, so we had to stop the night there. We had to offload the bags so that all passengers had access to their medications and general things required for overnight stays before they were taken to the hotels that had rooms available, not every passenger got a room.

"Before closing-up the aircraft, we checked everything in the cabin was switched off to avoid having flat batteries the following morning. Then we had to close the doors. Well, we're trained to close the doors from the inside, not from the outside. Us pilots tried to close the L2 door from the outside but without success, so we closed the L2 from the inside and exited the aircraft through the forward L1 door which fortunately we managed to close from the outside.

"The next morning with all passengers and bags on board when we were just about ready to go, we got a call from ops asking us to 'hold on, you've got one more customer to come'. We were sure we had all our passengers accounted for. Not so because the woman with the medical problem, who we had diverted to Gander for, arrived at the bottom of the steps ready to board the aircraft. Apparently, she had a bad case of indigestion. You can imagine the looks she got when she came up the steps and boarded! That proved to be an interesting experience. As a follow-on, once Virgin contracted MedLink to provide medical advice to crews when airborne, the number of diversions across the company's network decreased.

"After a Virgin Airbus A330 on a flight to Orlando returned to Gatwick with a suspected cargo fire, the aircraft had to be evacuated on the runway. The cabin crew did a good job and got all passengers safely off the aircraft, yet later that day one of the passengers appeared on

"On September 11, 2001, I was due to fly to Toronto. We pushed off the stand and taxied out and were good to go. Air traffic called to advise there was some sort of security incident going on and we needed to return to the stand."

a radio show complaining about the actions of the cabin crew. Because of the flight termination at Gatwick, Virgin tasked me to fly a 747 to take the customers to Orlando the next day. When the flight service manager made his initial announcement to the passengers, he remained composed and humourous when he said: "A warm welcome on this Virgin Atlantic flight to Orlando. Today, we will endeavour today to get you some way further than the M25 ring road. When the passenger who had made a TV appearance the previous day boarded the aircraft, nobody would talk to him because of what he said about the cabin crew – all the passengers thought they had done a fantastic job, which they had."

When Virgin Atlantic wanted to get some new publicity photographs of the 747, Bruce Stewart, the fleet captain at the time asked Peter to fly the aircraft in formation with a Jet Provost camera plane. Peter flew an aircraft from Manchester to an area near Manston in Kent to meet-up with the Jet Provost and conduct the photo shoot over the North Sea off the coast of Norfolk and Suffolk. The plan changed because the weather along the south coast turned out to be perfect for the photoshoot, so it was re-planned off the south coast to capture the cliffs in the backdrop of the photos.

Explaining the method to be used, Peter said: "At some point during a photo shoot, you have to bank the aircraft so the photographer can shoot images from underneath. I had to check which way Virgin was written underneath the aircraft to ensure the banks were flown the right way up. There were four of us onboard, Bruce as captain, me as first officer, another first officer, and one of our female cabin crew to ensure everything remained safely stowed throughout the cabins during the banking.

"So first, we did three approaches and go arounds at Manston so that other photographers could shoot from the ground, followed by the airborne element which involved the Jet Provost telling us what to do to get the best photos. The first set-up was flown with a nose-up pitch of about 45°. For the belly shots the 747 needed to be banked. On most modern aircraft, the 747 included, if you go above about 35°, the aircraft sends a bank angle warning. When we went to 60° of bank, the bank angle warning sounded repeatedly such that Bruce wanted to back-off a bit, but I said 'no, hold it there to get the shots'. Meanwhile, the cabin crew

was throwing up at the back of the flight deck because she'd never experienced anything like that flight condition before!"

JUMBO FEELING

Discussing what the 747 was like to fly, Peter said: "It is a big aircraft with lots of inertia and momentum, but a delight to fly. The flight controls are well harmonised and if you put her in an attitude and pointed her where you wanted her to go, she would go there, it was lovely and very stable on the approach.

"On the classic, you relied on the flight engineer for the radar altitude callouts. He would emphasise 35 feet because that was the point at which you flared the aircraft by adjusting your pitch attitude to settle nicely on the runway. One of the strange things about the classic - you could fly what appeared to be the same approach and flare at the same point one day, and you'd get on the runway real nice, and the next time you'd thump it down.

"She was hard work in a crosswind, and you really needed to know what you were doing, especially with the momentum in a 35-40kts

> **"The cabin crew was throwing up at the back of the flight deck because she'd never experienced anything like that flight condition before!"**

crosswind. When flying down the approach in those conditions you're tracking the main landing gear down the centre of the runway which means your position on the flight deck is almost over the edge of the runway.

"It's a great skill judging the flare. Generally, you kick off the drift and then input a lot of into-wind aileron control to make sure that the downward wing didn't drop. The big danger in a crosswind

landing was an engine pod impact. That was when you really earned your money. There was nothing more rewarding than gliding the aircraft on the rails with a 30kts crosswind and making a good landing, so it was a challenging but rewarding aircraft to fly."

Peter also reflected on the wonder of having a flight engineer as part of the crew on 747 classic models, he said: "Flight engineers knew so much about the aircraft. So, if anything did go wrong, they knew what they were doing. Flight engineers also had a knack for knowing so many handy things to make life easier when away from base. So, for example, they found out that the US Mail post office at New York/JFK had a fantastic kitchen that offered meals. Our engineers also found out that the US Mail chaps effectively wore very similar shirts to the ones we did, so if we took our epaulets off, we could a get breakfast for $3. In the days when we could host flight deck visits, on flights to Orlando kids would come on to the flight deck and one of the flight engineers wore Mickey Mouse gloves to brighten up their day." Socially and technically, they were worth their weight in gold."

Round-the-World Routes

Before Claude Zehran joined Cargolux 25 years ago he was an Airbus pilot. He undertook training with the Luxembourg-based airline to transition to the Boeing 747 which under the different design and operating philosophies required him to use his thumbs again to trim the Boeing monster. Today, Claude still flies the 747, and serves as the company's executive vice president of flight operations.

At the time Claude joined Cargolux, the company operated five 747-400 freighters on routes to Asia via the Middle East, today it has a fleet of 30. He completed ground school with the aid of computer-based trainers at the company's Luxembourg base and his simulator training overseas. The company commissioned its first simulator in 2000, and all subsequent sim training has been conducted in house.

Claude's first take-off and landing occurred on a flight between Dubai and Taipei, with a three-pilot crew. He didn't get out of his seat from take-off in Dubai, all the way to the landing in Taipei, and says he enjoyed "every single moment of the flight." He told the editor: "The landing was memorable because the flight deck seats are noticeably higher than other aircraft, so the approach was quite different as was knowing when to start the flare. When you start flying the 747 you have no way of understanding how

difficult it will be in terms of the force that you must utilise, but it's very easy to fly because it's so stable, and for its size, it's very agile."

747-8F

That flight to Taipei was on a 747-400. When the company announced it was ordering the 747-8F, Claude had recently joined the training department as a type rating instructor on the 400. There is no dedicated type rating for the 8 because it's a variant of the 400, so Claude was asked to evaluate the training offered for the 400. Explaining, he said: "All you need

is familiarisation training to be able to fly the 8. The scope of the training is limited but focuses on the major differences between the electronic checklists and the types of approach that can be flown based on the different navigation capabilities. We concluded that more training was required, and the decision was taken that the training department would produce an in-house training programme. Three pilots, all called Claude, were tasked with the job, which confused our Boeing colleagues who

were convinced that everybody in Luxembourg was called Claude. It took us six months to complete the training programme, after which we were considered so-called experts on the 8 which meant we gave many of the first training classes. We introduced electronic flight bags [EFBs] with the 8 and staged one class dedicated to using the EFB which was another difference compared to the 400. We used the first two 8 aircraft on short sectors to get as many pilots through as possible. It wasn't a

requirement to fly the aircraft to be qualified, but we decided it was beneficial to fly a couple of sectors with an experienced training captain to feel more comfortable operating the jet."

Claude's first 747-8 flight was from Luxembourg to Milan where the airport authority had organised a welcome ceremony with guests waiting on the apron. Rating the 8F very highly, Claude said: "The 747 gives any operator the best capabilities in terms of cargo volume and range. The wing and the engines are the first

Cargolux Boeing 747s seen at Luxembourg Airport. *Cargolux*

Boeing 747-400 LX-NCL is named after the biggest city in the north of Cargolux's home country of Luxembourg, Ettelbrück. The city holds the oldest local Christmas market in the central European nation. The aircraft is seen in a retro colour scheme. Cargolux

Boeing 747-400F LX-ECV parked at Shanghai Airport ready to load a Beluga whale for a special cargo charter flight to Reykjavik Airport in Iceland. The unusual load was transported in November 2019 on behalf of a foundation set-up to look after the two whales and the custom-built tanks were used to meet stringent animal welfare requirements. Cargolux

and foremost differences to the 400 though it's not much different to fly. The changes Boeing introduced on the 8 are helpful and added value to the aircraft while remaining close enough to the 400 such that you feel comfortable flying the 8 following only familiarisation training compared to a full type rating.

"The 747-8 enables you to fly different types of approaches, which allows us to fly into airports not available to the 400. Despite its higher weight and bigger cargo capability, you do not need a longer runway or better infrastructure, you can use any airport suitable for the 400 with one caveat, the added wingspan limits you in the use of taxiways and ultimately clearances to buildings and other aircraft so we must be very careful when manoeuvring on the ground.

"One major advantage of the 747-8 is its nose loading capability which is used regularly. The 747-8 was the last aircraft that offers this capability, any future cargo aircraft, at least in the foreseeable future, will not have nose loading capability. Nose loading allows you

> "It wasn't a requirement to fly the aircraft to be qualified, but we decided it was beneficial to fly a couple of sectors with an experienced training captain to feel more comfortable operating the jet."

to offload simultaneously in several locations on the aircraft. But the downside is that the nose of the aircraft is not as wide as the rest of the aircraft, so whatever pallets you want to load or unload through the nose need to be contoured. The upper corners must be shaped to suit the internal cargo bay, which reduces the volume on the upper part of a pallet by a couple of cubic metres. And any pallet loaded underneath the upper deck must be lower in

height to the pallets that are loaded aft of the upper deck. The nose loading door is operated by the loadmaster who uses a panel located next to the nose to open and close the nose door, a process that takes 45 seconds. The panel also controls the lighting. On the flight deck, the pilot has an indicator showing the status of the door, open or closed. There are 20 electrically powered bolts that lock the doors closed. If electrical power is lost to

Boeing 747-400F LX-VCV Monviso is operated by Cargolux Italia. Cargolux

Cargolux Boeing 747-8F LX-VCF featured a surgical mask design on the nose-cargo door along with the Luxembourg government's slogan 'Not without my mask', a testimony to Cargolux's on-going engagement in the fight against the global COVID-19 pandemic. Cargolux

the door system, the doors can be opened manually. There are certain wind speeds that when in effect the nose door must not be operated or left open.

"When you arrive at the aircraft, loading should be underway, so its power is on to be able to operate the loading system. The first thing you do is to initialise the inertial reference systems, there are three, to enable the aircraft to find its position, irrespective of satellites, that's a 10-minute job. You then check through the papers, so the flight plan, NOTAMs, weather conditions to determine the necessary fuel load so that fuelling can start which can take up to an hour. Then you check the systems, starting with the overhead panel to see that the systems

are in the correct state for flight. Next you prepare the flight management computer and enter the route, then prepare your departure performance based on the weight of the aircraft, the position of the aircraft's centre of gravity and current meteorological conditions, to determine the thrust setting and flap setting you will require for take-off. These requirements are independently checked by the first officer. The pilot in charge of flying the aircraft will brief the other pilots and ensure that they have a mutual understanding of what they are going to do. This is followed by the walkaround to visually check that the aircraft is in an overall good state, which completes the ground procedures. You then wait for the maintenance

engineer to bring you the technical logbook, to learn about the status of the aircraft and if there are any items that you need to consider for the flight or for the aircraft's performance. When loading is complete, the loadmaster will come to the flight deck to advise you of that. Once those the two procedures are complete, you receive a sheet to confirm your take-off performance, then wait for the doors to close, then pushback and start the engines."

CARGOLUX OPERATIONS

Cargolux operates from its one base in Luxembourg but the cargo capacity of the 747 is such that it is not always possible to fly to a destination, completely fill the aircraft

A Cargolux Boeing 747-8F undergoes de-icing at Oslo International airport. Erik Moen

The first Boeing 747-400 freighter for Cargolux, LX-ECV, prior to the final body join on Boeing's Everett production line. Boeing

Two Boeing 747-400F aircraft parked nose-to-nose for a promotional photoshoot. Cargolux

and return to Luxembourg. Explaining how its operations work, Claude said: "Cargo loads are not equal both ways but unilateral, so when flying from Asia to Europe and from Asia to America, you don't have the same volumes as you do when flying from Europe to Asia or from America to Asia. Intermediate stops are required to optimise use of the cargo capacity to its max. An aircraft with

400 passengers on board has a capacity to carry around 40 tonnes of cargo which is nothing for a freighter aircraft, generally we try to take-off with at least 110 tonnes of cargo on board. That means our endurance and our range is shorter than a passenger version which can fly much further in one hop because they are lighter and have a bigger fuel capacity than a cargo version. In general,

freighters fly on shorter routes with technical stops in between.

"All Cargolux flights start in Luxembourg and return there either on direct routes or via a technical stop. We also fly routes from Luxembourg, head east, go around the world and fly back from the west. From a Far East destination like Hong Kong or Singapore we fly to Anchorage, Alaska for a technical stop

Cargolux's first Boeing 747-400 LX-ECV parked at the Luxembourg cargo centre following its delivery flight from Boeing's facility at King County Airport in Seattle, Washington. Cargolux

> ""When you arrive at the aircraft, loading should be underway, so its power is on to be able to operate the loading system."

and onto any of our destinations in America - Seattle, Los Angeles, Chicago, Indianapolis, Houston, New York, or Miami - and then back to Luxembourg. This helps to keep the operational costs under control. In this typical example, the cargo would likely be completely offloaded in the Far East and a new load flown to the United States. Flying east from Luxembourg mainly serves the purpose of carrying freight from the Far East to the United States. Similarly, flying back to Luxembourg serves the purpose of carrying cargo to Europe.

"When you make a technical stop you only offload part of the load, so one challenge is to place the pallets that will be offloaded at the next destination close to a cargo door, so you don't have to offload the whole aircraft just to get to two pallets which minimises the turnaround. That's an aspect that our ground logistics department needs to keep under control because you can lose an enormous amount of time."

Discussing what aspects weigh heaviest on his mind when flying a route, Claude said: "Airport arrival can be challenging. We used to fly to Quito Mariscal Sucre international airport in Ecuador, which was in a valley with three volcanoes nearby. The field's elevation had an impact on your approach speed, which has

Cargolux

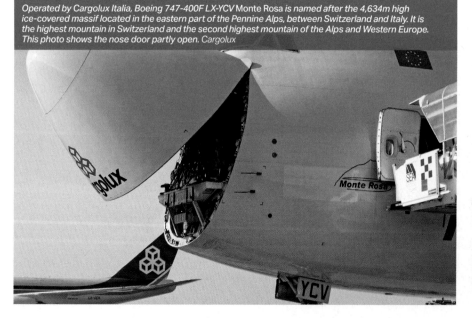

Retired from Cargolux service in September 1995, Boeing 747-200F LX-DCV in flight. Cargolux

Operated by Cargolux Italia, Boeing 747-400F LX-YCV Monte Rosa is named after the 4,634m high ice-covered massif located in the eastern part of the Pennine Alps, between Switzerland and Italy. It is the highest mountain in Switzerland and the second highest mountain of the Alps and Western Europe. This photo shows the nose door partly open. Cargolux

Brandishing the Car50lux slogan on the underside of the nose door applied to mark the airline's 50th anniversary in May 2020. Cargolux

an impact on the required runway length, so a challenging operation. We also encounter such challenges in our charter operation, which is a significant part of the business. Recently, we had a charter flight to carry the Solar Impulse long-range experimental solar-powered aircraft to Stennis airport in Louisiana. Stennis had never received a 747 before. Such an operation requires thorough preparation, and you must be prepared to deal with the little unknown hiccups that you might encounter during the operation.

"Cargolux operates both scheduled and charter services. The differences between the two types of service really depend on the departure airport and the destination airport, the speciality of the cargo and the attention it requires. The destination airport can make a significant difference, especially if the location is unfamiliar with the Boeing 747 and large cargo operations. Greater preparations are required which include giving briefings to the flight deck crew and cargo handlers about what to expect. Cargolux scheduled services are just like a passenger airline, season by season, and the company offers capacity for charters. A charter flight is usually required to meet increased demand of an entity or to transport a special cargo load to a specific destination. In 2019 Cargolux carried two Beluga whales from Shanghai to Iceland on behalf of a foundation set up to look after the two whales and was staged to meet stringent animal welfare requirements."

Explaining the complicated arrangements required to transport two giant aquatic mammals, Claude said: "We developed two bespoke containers each to carry a whale, equipment to adjust water levels and to filter the water. Limited to eight persons onboard, we had three pilots, three veterinarians and two engineers. The challenge was to avoid water spillage out of the tanks and into the electronics compartment. We took off and landed with the minimum water level required to carry the weight of each whale. The water level was adjusted after take-off to make each whale more comfortable. We spent months planning the flight."

Reflecting on the jumbo, Claude said the 747 is part of the history of Cargolux: "We were the first operator to fly the 400 freighter, the launch customer for the 747-8 freighter and first in the world to operate it. The success of Cargolux and the 747 are closely linked. It's not the most modern aircraft anymore and we are buying Boeing 777 freighters to replace are oldest 747-400s, but it's called the 'Queen of the Skies' for a reason and a lot of pilots like to fly that aircraft because of its uniqueness."

> "An aircraft with 400 passengers on board has a capacity to carry around 40 tonnes of cargo which is nothing for a freighter aircraft, generally we try to take-off with at least 110 tonnes of cargo on board."

TriStars, A340s and Boeing 747s

Having flown 4,000 hours with the Royal Air Force on TriStar aircraft, Paul Singleton joined Virgin Atlantic in 2005 to continue his flying career. At the time Virgin was operating the Airbus A340 and the 747, there was only one choice for Paul, the jumbo.

When Paul started flying the Boeing 747-400 as part of his conversion course with Virgin Atlantic, he found the aircraft's handling to be similar to that of his previous mount, the Lockheed L-1011 TriStar.

He started line flying with Virgin Atlantic in early 2006 and flew as a first officer for 12 years. During that period, the company decided to ask first officers to become trainers. Paul successfully applied and received his type rating instructor qualification in late 2013 and spent the remainder of his time as first officer, alternating between flying as a line first officer and instructing in the simulator. Paul was subsequently given command as a captain, and after a short period made-up to training captain.

The COVID-19 pandemic forced Virgin Atlantic to lay off most of its pilots, including Paul who then landed a job with a cargo airline flying 747-400 freighters. He hauled cargo for 18 months before rejoining Virgin on the A330 in the spring of 2022.

Turning the clock back to his first line flight, Paul recalled: "The first time I flew a jumbo jet was with 390 passengers on board going from Heathrow to Boston, Massachusetts, all my training had been completed in the simulator. Because I'd already flown the TriStar, another heavy jet, I qualified under the zero-flight time scheme which meant I could do all my training in the simulator, including circuit training, and landing training. Consequently, under the zero-flight time scheme, the first time you take-off with passengers on board is the first time you've ever taken off in the 747. It was quite a feeling to be sat in the right-hand seat of a jumbo jet knowing I'd never flown one before and was about to fly it with 390 passengers

on board. That's quite a thing. Seven or so hours after taking off from Heathrow, I carried out my first ever landing in a 747 on Boston-Logan Airport's runway, which was also quite something."

Despite the success Paul had achieved to that date, there's a tragic association to his first 747 flight. The captain that day was Mark Naylor, who Paul described as "a wonderful man and a wonderful instructor." Mark tragically passed away in April 2008.

Paul's line training comprised 12 sectors, so, six return flights. If the pilot is deemed ready at the end of that programme, they fly a check flight to certify they're ready to fly the line as a fully qualified pilot. Once again, Paul got to fly to Boston for his line check. It went well and he was released to line flying. He described his release to line flying as "a milestone you never forget."

Recalling his emotions as he travelled down the runway for take-off at Heathrow, Paul said:

Boeing 747-41R G-VXLG Ruby Tuesday touches down at Las Vegas McCarran International Airport after a non-stop flight from Heathrow. Chris Wood

The flight deck of a Boeing 747-400. Chris Wood

"Under the zero-flight time scheme, the first time you take-off with passengers on board is the first time you've ever taken off in the 747."

"The captain must be a type rating instructor, and not a line training captain. Because the student is in full control, the captain must be sufficiently skilled that if something goes wrong, they've been trained to intervene in a timely manner so that they can keep the aircraft safe. There was a lot going on so probably more concentration than excitement because you can't be distracted by what's going on around, you absolutely must be on your metal because there are procedures to follow. Only the captain can abort the take-off, but after the stop-go speed is reached, you've got to be able to control the aircraft in the event of a critical engine loss, get airborne, keep the aircraft flying, climb away from the ground and operate the aircraft safely despite bells and whistles going off in the flight deck. There's obviously a lot to take in and your concentration level is high."

Comparing reality to the simulator, Paul said: "The simulator was very good, but it couldn't replicate momentum and the feeling that you get in a real aeroplane as you accelerate down the runway. As the aeroplane gets to a certain speed it feels unstoppable and wants to fly. Once you get to 'V rotate' the aircraft almost leaps into the sky, and you don't get the feeling of a massive sluggish beast. Far from it, Boeing build aeroplanes that handle nicely, they are pilot's aeroplanes. So, the difference I guess with four engines

coming up rather than three on a TriStar is that there are more visual cues, and your hand grip is much wider, because there are four thrust levers rather than three.

"The 747 feels like an incredibly powerful aeroplane, as it rolls down the runway, above 100kts it accelerates very well, especially with a lighter fuel payload for a shorter flight to Boston compared to Los Angeles. Once it lifts off the ground, it's delightful. The controls are very light. Once you get past V1 and you've rotated the aircraft off the runway, your concern reduces because you're now in the air and if anything goes wrong in the air it's a little bit easier to fly, because it's going faster, and the rudders are more effective. The big concern is losing an engine. But given that you've got a lot of airflow over the rudder, you don't need as much rudder to control an engine failure after take-off as you would for an engine failure during take-off. The climb-out routine involves lots of radio calls and responding to the instructions given by air traffic control, listening carefully to what they're asking you to do. Then you get to manipulate the aircraft autopilot to select one of two ways to climb, you can do it manually or by flight level change via VNAV."

Vertical Navigation or VNAV is an autopilot mode that allows the aircraft to adjust vertical speed to meet a predetermined altitude at a specified waypoint.

Close-up of the left instrument panel on a Boeing 747-400. Chris Wood

"During the first hour of flight after take-off from Heathrow, you're preparing to put the aircraft into oceanic airspace, which is all procedural flying, so there are quite a lot of checks that you've got to do, applying for clearances across the Atlantic, checking you've got the right waypoints input into the navigation kit, checking the aircraft systems, getting the weather to make sure that anywhere you need to divert to is usable before you go on to the Atlantic. Ten minutes past the oceanic entry waypoint you start to relax and enjoy the view."

Paul's first landing at Boston was really business as usual given his TriStar experience. "It wasn't a novelty but quite different from the TriStar because of geometry. The geometry of a 747 means that as you execute the flare manoeuvre to arrest your rate of descent to land, the pilot's eye height [eye-to-wheel height] in a jumbo jet is about 75 feet, whereas the corresponding eye height on a TriStar is about 20 feet lower, so the runway looks a little different. The 747 is 231 feet long and the TriStar is 165 feet long, so 70 feet longer, so you've got to be aware of where the aircraft is in relation to the runway threshold. In smaller aeroplanes you aim for the runway threshold to put the aircraft down, but if you did that in a jumbo jet, you would put the wheels through the fence at the end of the runway.

"Landing in a jumbo happens quite quickly because the 747 aircraft is flying an approach speed six or seven knots faster than a TriStar of similar weight, because despite being heavier, it's got bigger wings producing more lift. So, as you're coming into land in a 747, you learn the visual cues needed to start the landing manoeuvre, which you only get from flying real

"Only the captain can abort the take-off, but after the stop-go speed is reached, you've got to be able to control the aircraft in the event of a critical engine loss, get airborne, keep the aircraft flying, climb away from the ground and operate the aircraft safely despite bells and whistles going off in the flight deck."

aeroplanes, because as good as the simulator is, it's not real life and the graphics are not quite the same as looking at a runway with your eyes. It was exciting, flaring for the runway and making sure that you don't float and keeping it straight. There was no cross wind on my first landing in Boston, it was benign weather. It's an exciting thing to land a jumbo jet.

"The next milestone after you've started line flying is the first recurrent check taken in the simulator which tests what you've learned from six months of flying the line consolidating your knowledge and flying technique. Virgin Atlantic's training department has always been exceptionally good. They've always been very fair, very helpful. Although there's a little bit of trepidation when you go into the simulator, the idea is that you come out of the simulator feeling a little more confident about the more difficult aspects of flying a big jet with, for example, strong crosswinds, wind shear, and aircraft system failures. Although there is a little bit of trepidation, it's only because you don't know what's coming your way. You don't know what emergency scenarios the instructor is going to present to you, and you hope that your skills will be up to it. The more times you go into the simulator, the better you get.

"As you fly more and more you consolidate your knowledge of the aircraft which helps with your judgement and decision making when confronted with an issue. For example, when you arrive at the aircraft to take it flying, the engineers might advise you that the hydraulic backup system is not working. On a jumbo, each hydraulic system is powered by an engine. Each engine powers a gearbox, which

Virgin Atlantic Airways Boeing 747-443 G-VGAL Jersey Girl at London-Gatwick International Airport. Chris Wood

drives the hydraulic system gearbox itself and pressurises the system and [is] therefore available for use. If an engine fails there's a backup system, which for the biggest systems is driven by air and on the smaller systems is driven by an electric pump. But if for some reason your hydraulic backup system had failed, you can still dispatch the aeroplane with a backup system failure, but there are procedures that you must use to mitigate what would happen if the engine then failed, because you would then lose hydraulic power because there's no backup system to bring the hydraulic system back. So, you're not getting airborne with an unserviceable system, you're getting airborne with an unserviceable backup to

that system. In accordance with the minimum equipment list, you're allowed to do that.

"The number one and number four hydraulic systems power the most important aircraft services, the landing gears, flaps, slats, and brakes. So, if you lost the number one engine and its hydraulic system you would not be able to retract the landing gear you would then depend on the backup system. So, in your performance calculations you have to assume that the number one engine is going to fail, and you will lose that hydraulic system – a worst case scenario – and therefore a procedure that has to be put in place. So, you need to know such procedures to be able to get around such issues, which becomes

corporate knowledge through the years rather than knowledge that's in the books."

BECOMING A TRAINER

During Paul's line flying days as a first officer, the company put out a notice advising that it was accepting applications from first officers to become trainers. Paul applied and went through an interview process which included a presentation given to a panel. Paul chose to speak about the 747's fuel system and the things that could go wrong. His presentation focussed on the freeze points of fuel and the calculation required to determine a freeze point of a fuel payload comprising, for example some American fuel left over from the flight back to Heathrow (loaded

Boeing 747-41R G-VXLG Ruby Tuesday seen on take-off from Las Vegas McCarran International Airport. Chris Wood

Mustang Sally, *Boeing 747-41R G-VROC in Virgin Atlantic Airways'
colours at Los Angeles International Airport. Chris Wood*

at a US airport) and some European (loaded at
Heathrow). The freeze point of American fuel is
minus 40°C, whereas European fuel is minus 47°C.

Explaining, Paul said: "You had to work out
what fuel was left at the end of the flight.
Normally between the four outer fuel tanks
located in the area of the wing where it is
thinnest and the place where the atmospheric
temperature is going to affect the temperature
of the fuel the most. For example, if we started
with ten tonnes of American Jet A fuel onboard,
two and a half tonnes in each of the four tanks,
and we then loaded 70-80 tonnes of Jet A1
European fuel with a lower freeze point, 12.2
tonnes per tank, we would calculate the ratio.
In this example the ratio of Jet A to Jet A1 will
be two and a half tonnes against 12.2 tonnes,
which is the maximum you can put in the outer
tanks. Then you use a fuel blending table to
work out a freeze point for that blend of fuel.

I chose one of the panel members, a flight
crew manager, a non-pilot, to teach how to
do this, and then come up with the answer to
demonstrate that I could teach people how
to do things that they didn't already know.
My presentation must have been judged as
reasonable because I was selected as one of
six training officers.

"Initially, the six of us were supposed to
be used mainly to do classroom teaching for
new joiners and prepare presentations for the
simulator, teaching in the ground environment
rather than onboard an aeroplane. For
whatever reason, Virgin decided that two of
us were to become type rating instructors,
one of whom was me. This meant doing the
type rating instructors course, which is very
difficult. The first week, part one, you're taught
how to teach, how to prepare classroom
presentations, how to do a board brief. The

second week, part two, was devoted to how
you teach in the simulator, which is also tough.

"The first event each day involved presenting
a brief with your colleague to the two tutors
that were teaching us. They then debrief each
of you on your presentation. Then you go into a
simulator to teach an exercise to the tutors who
play the part of student pilots. Once the exercise
is complete you debrief the students to see how
you think it went. Then you're debriefed by the
tutors, on how your performance was. All that
takes an entire day, then it's time to prepare for
the next day's lesson plan together. You then
present to each other that night and start the
following morning with another presentation
followed by another simulator session and
debriefs. It's an absolutely exhausting two weeks."

Paul then explained the difficulties of
learning to instruct: "You must find a way to
interrogate your students in a way that allows

Virgin Atlantic Airways Boeing 747-41R G-VAST *Ladybird* at Glasgow International Airport. *Chris Wood*

Photographed against a dark sky, Virgin Atlantic Airways Boeing 747-41R G-VWOW Cosmic Girl on take-off from London-Heathrow. Chris Wood

Sitting in the sun at Antigua V.C. Bird International Airport, Virgin Atlantic Airways' Boeing 747-41R G-VAST Ladybird ahead of its return flight to London-Heathrow. Chris Wood

them to feel free to express what they think they did well, and what they think they perhaps could have done better. But you can't just ask them a question where the answer could be yes, or no. You need to ask open questions. For example, you've just done an exercise and you think it's gone well. Take five minutes to think of two things that you did well together today and one thing that perhaps you could have done better? That instantly becomes a discussion rather than just one- or two-word answer as to how it went. It's called facilitation. At that point, the instructor can either choose to sit back and allow them to talk amongst themselves and take notes or you facilitate the discussion by saying things like, okay, Dave, Caroline was the captain today, tell me two things about Caroline's style that you found made life easy for you, which sparks the discussion. You're like a sheepdog. The idea is you keep the discussion going, and you guide the discussion into the direction you want to go, because it could be something that as the instructor you

want to talk about that they haven't done well. But you must allow them to fully develop the discussion whilst you facilitate the direction that it is going in. That's quite a skill to learn. As is the ability to jump into the opposite seat and demonstrate to the student what you want them to do when they are not grasping the concepts and do that to a sufficiently high standard, so they absorb your instruction and feel comfortable to have another go.

"On the final day, you complete a simulator session that involves everything you've done over the two weeks, only this time, you have an examiner watching over you, who grades you and lets you know if you've passed. Once you've successfully finished the course you are a qualified ground-based first officer, at that level you're not allowed to train in the air, you must be the commander of the aeroplane to do that. You're then rostered on the simulator schedule to instruct line pilot first officers, trying to facilitate their further development. It's quite a skill and the more you do it, the better

you become at doing it. Then with time, you try to garner a reputation for being fair, good, and knowledgeable, all the things you want your instructor to be. It's a hugely rewarding role, giving pilots confidence in an activity, or teaching them how to conduct an activity, helping them to achieve their potential."

TAKING COMMAND
From a career perspective, Paul's next milestone was the biggest one of all, his command upgrade. In upgrading a pilot to command, the company wants to know that they are capable of taking command of the aircraft and ensuring that they are going to protect the aeroplane, the crew, the passengers, and the brand. The selection process involves a one-day interview and a day in the simulator. If successful, the candidate takes the command course.

Recalling his command course Paul said: "It involved six simulators. The first two are to get used to being in the captain's seat, learning

"In smaller aeroplanes you aim for the runway threshold to put the aircraft down, but if you did that in a jumbo jet, you would put the wheels through the fence at the end of the runway."

how to fly with your other hand, but then very quickly, introduction of some complicated scenarios which, as commander, you need to be able to deal with. The big one is the sixth simulator session when you're presented with a scenario where time becomes less and less and the need to get on the ground becomes greater. That could be anything from the aircraft deteriorating around you, to being in a really bad weather environment or having a passenger deteriorate to the point where you've got to get on the ground.

"The first time you go to work wearing four stripes and lots of gold braid on your hat, it's all on you, everybody's looking to you for direction and leadership. On my first route as captain, we were over Canada en route Orlando when a problem with the

pressurisation system popped-up. Regulating valves for the pressurisation system have two modes of action, automatic and manual. You're allowed to dispatch with one or two valves not working which we had done. An outer valve controller had failed. So effectively, if it failed and ran away closed, so we would find it hard to depressurise the aircraft and if it failed and ran away open, the aircraft would start depressurising by itself straight away.

"First, we went to manual pressurisation which meant one of the two pilots was always engaged in making sure that the outflow valve position was such that the aircraft remained at the required pressurisation to the altitude we were at, which then made life difficult on the approach because that's the point at which the aircraft automatically starts to reduce the cabin altitude. I flew the approach while the first officer was heavily involved with manually moving the outflow valves to maintain the pressurisation that we needed. We chose 10,000ft as the altitude that we would depressurise the aircraft, which is the safe altitude, so that the first officer wouldn't be working to near capacity on the approach when we needed to be working together, monitoring me rather than worrying about where the aircraft pressurisation schedule was. The physiological effects on your body as you descend from 10,000ft reasonably quickly down to ground level is a lot worse when the aircraft's depressurised because the aircraft cabin depressurises at a slower rate to make it more comfortable on your sinuses and inner ear.

> "So, you're not getting airborne with an unserviceable system, you're getting airborne with an unserviceable backup to that system. In accordance with the minimum equipment list, you're allowed to do that."

Virgin Atlantic Airways Boeing 747-4Q8 G-VBIG Tinker Belle *lands on San Francisco International Airport's runway 28L at the end of a long flight from London Heathrow.* Chris Wood

"On another, the cabin crew said they got a sensation of an acrid smell in the cabin, which obviously in an aeroplane is not good. We were coming back from Las Vegas on a land track across most of the continental United States, so diversion airports were always within 20 minutes diversion time. If we'd been over the ocean, it would have been very uncomfortable. We made decision points. If there were no more sensations of smoke or acrid smell by the time we reached the eastern seaboard of the United States, it was safe to assume we had dealt with the problem and we could take the aircraft all the way back, which is what we ended up doing. The problem was found to be the plastic casing around the fan heater in the back of an oven, which the crew shut down. The casing had warped so the fan itself was catching on it which caused friction and the heating up.

"When something happens, as the first officer you look left toward the captain to see what they want to do about it. When you are the captain, if you look left, you catch your own reflection and you realise you must make the decision. But we don't make decisions by ourselves. The whole point of command is that you are the chairman of the board. The board consists of yourself and the other pilot or pilots with inputs from any source that you care to take. You're encouraged to consider everyone on the aircraft as a potential source of help, including passengers who may spot something on the wing such as de-icing fluid or a partially deployed spoiler panel. As the commander you're there to collate all the information and facilitate a discussion as to the course of action, and then decide what to do next once you've got the support of everybody involved."

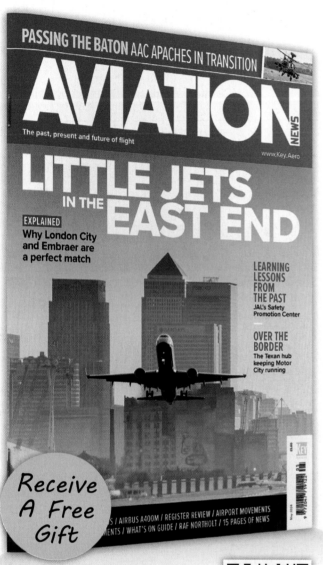

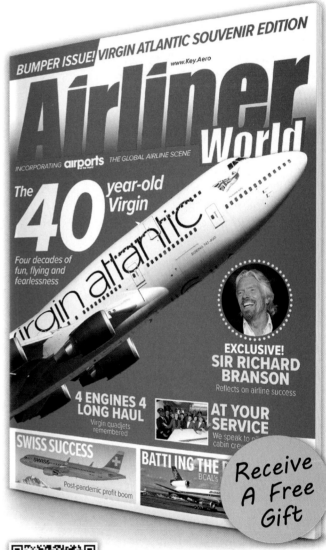

Rivet Joint to Jumbo

Chester Wolfe started his flying career with the US Air Force. After graduating from the Specialized Undergraduate Pilot Training programme, he flew the T-1 Jayhawk trainer as an instructor followed by the RC-135 Rivet Joint reconnaissance aircraft. After leaving the USAF, Chester trained for his airline transport pilot certificate and joined Kalitta Air in 2018.

Chester Wolfe went through Kalitta's in house training programme for the Boeing 747-400 and made his first flight as a first officer in June 2018. Three years later he was upgraded to captain. If the reader is unfamiliar with Kalitta Air, Connie Kalitta, a drag racer, and a National Hot Rod racing associate, formed Connie Kalitta Air Services in 1967

flying car parts for the large US automobile manufacturers in the state of Michigan, using a Cessna 310. In 1997 he formed Kalitta Air. The company's headquarters is at Willow Run Airport in Ypsilanti, Michigan and operates its own maintenance facility at Oscoda Airport, the former Wurtsmith Air Force Base.

For company pilots like Chester, Ypsilanti is considered the home base, but they are all home based and use a domicile airport from where they fly to a destination where their 747 aircraft is located. The company issues a bid

list in the middle of each month. Senior pilots get first choice followed by the junior ranks. The bid list is the basis for the company's flight schedule and the trips individual pilots will fly. Explaining the system, Chester said: "Some of the trips are a straight block which means you're working from this time to this time, but you don't know exactly where you're going to be. Other trips may be planned to start at, for example New York-JFK, but operationally, because the aeroplane is not making JFK on time, the company may adjust and start your trip in Miami

Kalitta Air Boeing 747-221(F) N748CK seen on take-off from Los Angeles International Airport on July 30, 2013. *Chris Wood*

A view of the northern lights from the flight deck of a Boeing 747 freight. *Kalitta Air/Ron Lambert*

Ramp services technicians unload cargo from a Kalitta Air Boeing 747 aircraft at Dover Air Force Base, Delaware. US Air Force/Senior Airman Christopher Quail

> "Some trips are split, such that you go out for eight days, then have a week at home, and then go out for another eight days."

for his first flight. Recalling the day, Chester said: "The first day is about figuring out where exactly you fit in with the rest of the crew and knowing your duties to support the captain. On operational experience missions, as first officer, you do most of the flying, so it's really front loaded for learning how to interact with the aeroplane itself. She talks to you all the time, so you have to learn her language. Then when you put an input in, there's an expected outcome. If you don't get that outcome, you need to ask yourself, did I do something wrong? It's most likely you did, or you didn't input what you thought you were doing, so the

system is not behaving the way you thought it was. And if you did input what you thought you were doing, it's likely you're not understanding what's happening and how the system works. You really need to get comfortable with recognising what the flight mode is doing and at what time, to understand how to put the aeroplane where you want it and what you need to do to achieve that.

"It's a matter of getting used to how the aeroplane works and how it flies itself. Because of the initial learning curve, a lot of people suffer from a degree of lack in confidence because you don't want to mess something

instead. Most trips are about 16 days in length. Some trips are split, such that you go out for eight days, then have a week at home, and then go out for another eight days. There's a myriad of things that drive the schedule. But for the most part, it's pretty much two weeks on two weeks off. And based on your seniority and the preferences you put in, it may be exactly that, or it may be closer to two weeks on, a week off, and two weeks on. But then the following month, you'll have three weeks off because of how you manipulate your schedule. If you can manipulate your schedule and you're willing to put up with, say, a back-to-back trip and be out for almost 30 days, maybe you can work to have a month off without even taking a vacation. Then if you take a month off for vacation, you can potentially have eight to 10 weeks off."

FIRST TRIP

After completing his simulator training, and passing his simulator check ride, Chester was qualified as a 747 first officer and ready

The Boeing 747-400 wing has a sweep angle of 37.5° which helps the aircraft to cruise efficiently. US Air Force/Senior Airman Zachary Cacicia

up. For example, when a pilot disengages the autopilot on approach, sometimes, they will leave the auto-throttles engaged, and that bites you, depending on the wind conditions and the approach. As a pilot gets more confident, and I tell first officers this all the time, turn the auto-throttles off and fly the aeroplane, like you ought to fly the aeroplane and you'll be amazed how easy it is. It's easy to control provided you keep her on speed.

"During landing, you're reliant on the GPS call out as you descend, 50, 40, 30 etc and if you're methodical and mechanical about how you start reducing your power to set up your flare, in the beginning, it takes a little bit of time to get used to.

"On operational experience flying, as first officer you do most of the flying and landings. The instructor will fly and while doing so checks that you know how to monitor the pilot and what the duties are. You must also be familiar with the duties of being the relief pilot. Much of my operational experience was gained flying in and out of Istanbul on short trips to major cities around Europe and North Africa, and by the end of that phase, I was pretty good at landing the 747. When the aircraft is at 50ft, I slowly reduce power, and then slowly raise the nose up at a descent rate so when it reaches the flare position, the aircraft should be about 20 to 30ft in the air, and then just let it settle for a smooth landing. That said, some landings are rougher than others whether intentional or unintentional. The hardest part is just getting the dang thing on centreline, it's just so big. It's hard to

Airmen from the 436th Aerial Port Squadron based at Dover Air Force Base, Delaware load cargo onto a Kalitta Air Boeing 747.
US Air Force/Senior Airman Zachary Cacicia

A marshaller directs a Kalitta Air 747 at Dover Air Force Base, Delaware. US Air Force/Senior Airman Christopher Quail

imagine that when you're landing, it weighs 650,000lb, the wind is blowing, and you must keep the aeroplane where it needs to be. Despite its size and weight, it's still affected by winds just like anything else."

When it was time for Chester to take-off in a 747 for the first time, he had already completed numerous take offs in a simulator. "So, you're used to [the principle], but taking of for real is new and there's a rush. You feel like you're hanging on to the tail. There's a lot of stuff happening and you're trying to keep to the required procedures as much as possible. On your first take-off, your instructor will make sure that you're doing what you need to do. But it was a thrill, particularly when you're flying it and doing a full power take-off. You hear the engines start to growl and feel the power as you're lumbering down the runway slowly accelerating. You see the end of the runway getting closer and you know the aircraft should rotate soon but you're not quite at speed yet, but then once you rotate, it lifts off easy and flies. It's an amazing aircraft, and I'm always happy after take-off because it just feels so good, even after all these years."

Discussing his first landing, Chester said: "I was probably more frazzled for the first landing than the first take-off because you're concentrating on keeping everything controlled and getting off the ground, and not scraping the tail. There's no tail skid on a 747 so it's possible to scrape the tail. The landing comes quick, and even if you've flown an aeroplane that lands that fast, the 747's average approach speed is 150-160kts, so you're talking two to 2.5 miles per minute, so the last four to five miles takes under two minutes and you're on the ground. You're very reliant on the flight director, but once you go visual, you rely on your instinct to flare the aircraft for a smooth and easy

touchdown Because the aeroplane is easy to land, if you keep it within parameters, it's not a problem. From my own experience, my first good landing when you have competence and know what you're doing was more memorable than my first."

PICKING UP AN AEROPLANE
Kalitta Air pilots receive their trip schedule the day prior to the flight departure. Sometimes the schedule stays the same, sometimes it changes by the hour as things happen. Providing some examples, Chester said: "You're supposed to be leaving at two in the morning, then suddenly, you're leaving now, at 10 o'clock the day after, or your schedule is suddenly blank, and you're waiting for your schedule to be reworked to catch up for events that have happened. You'll get picked up from the hotel about two and a half hours

Kalitta Air/Ron Lambert

"The first day is about figuring out where exactly you fit in with the rest of the crew and knowing your duties to support the captain."

Boeing 747-4B5F N702CK parked on the ramp at Ted Stevens Anchorage Airport with the snow-covered Chugach Mountains in the distant background. Kalitta Air/Ron Lambert

prior to the scheduled departure depending on the location, how much processing you must go through at the airport, so it takes a while to process. If you're in a foreign country, of course, you must process out of immigration and go to security.

"Then there are places, like Anchorage, for example, where we are driven straight to the aeroplane. The gate guard checks to make sure that we're on the list, checks the driver and then we're dropped off at the bottom of stairs, take your bags on board and stow them. On average, our flights are seven or eight hours. Kalitta flies one route from Cincinnati to Incheon, South Korea. That's about 15 hours,

so you've got to make sure that there's enough food on board and appropriate bedding for the bunks used by the crew for sleeping during en route rest periods.

"If it's a tech stop, you get either fuel or change the crew but there is no loading or unloading operations. If loading is involved but the deck is empty you start thinking about the potential delay while the aircraft is loaded. Once on board the aircraft the biggest part of the captain's job is stay informed and to coordinate the other folks involved. For example, the captain speaks with the loadmaster about the required fuel load. One hundred thousand pounds of fuel takes 40-60

minutes to upload so we need to make sure that fuelling the aircraft gets done ahead of time. He also speaks with the engineer about the aeroplane's maintenance status. If there's a minor issue, I ask them to keep an eye on it.

"Once the discussions are complete, the flight deck crew starts to pre-flight the aeroplane with the expectation that the captain gets everything coordinated on time. If not, you call the company and discuss the issues. You might have a maintenance delay or an issue with loading the cargo. With the latter, do you wait for the cargo or leave without it? Generally, you wait for the cargo and accept the delay, but there have been times when it's

Kalitta Air Boeing 747-4B5F N706CK takes off from Ted Stevens Anchorage Airport on a balmy June afternoon. Chris Wood

been an issue, and you have to leave. If you've got hazardous cargo on board, you must know what the material is, where it's positioned and take note of any other additional measures which might dictate the routing. For example, you are not permitted to fly with explosives over Ireland.

"You coordinate the final fuel load and tell the loadmaster for their weight and balance calculation. A lot of the freight forwarders operate in kilogrammes, and we operate in pounds, so we must make sure the gross weight is converted properly, the number looks right, and it makes sense. The loadmaster confirms when the loading is complete and gives me a briefing. You receive a weight and balance, either electronically through the ACARS system, or handed to me on paper. You then verify the weight and balance against the flight plan to make sure the load is within limits.

If you have a higher-than-expected weight, you need to coordinate with the company to run a new flight plan, because the higher load may adjust fuel burn, where you can land in the event of an emergency, or even prohibit us from take-off. You make the final verification check, get an update on the weather and coordinate with maintenance to make sure that nothing new has popped up on the aeroplane, then you decide when we go within the departure window. If it's too late, for example, the situation may require some coordination, particularly if there's a slot time at the airport of arrival."

DUTY DAY
For a 15-hour flight between Cincinnati and Incheon additional crew are required, a standard three-person flight crew is only allowed to fly for so long. Standard Federal Aviation Administration rules dictate that

Cargo handlers load a specialised pallet on to a Boeing 747-400 via the nose loading door. *Kalitta Air*

"Much of my operational experience was gained flying in and out of Istanbul on short trips to major cities around Europe and North Africa, and by the end of that phase, I was pretty good at landing the 747."

a pilot cannot be at the controls for more than eight hours. That predicates the crew complement.

Explaining the different crew complements, Chester said: "The company has three categories of crew, a basic crew which is two pilots, a standard crew has three pilots, and a double crew has four. It might be one captain, three first officers, it might be two captains and two first officers. If a duty day is expected to be over 20 hours, then we're supposed to have two captains and two first officers. Most of the time, you have a mechanic on board, and you may have a loadmaster depending on the nature of the flight. If it's a military flight, for example, you'll have a company loadmaster on board.

"With three pilots you normally start to break right after level off, which usually takes about 20 minutes which is when you start your calculations to figure out how long the break is going to be. You end the breaks about an hour before arrival. With a three-person crew, you divide it by three, and then between you decide which break we're going to take. You usually give the landing pilot priority, let him pick first. With a double crew, you evenly split the flight time in half or on the 15-hour flight between Cincinnati and Incheon even breaks are about six and a half hours. Some pilots don't sleep for six and a half hours so we may

On board a Kalitta Air Boeing 747-400 high above the clouds loaded with hundreds of thousands of pounds of cargo kept aloft by the power of four Pratt & Whitney turbofan engines and a super-efficient wing. *Kalitta Air/Ron Lambert*

do a short break of one and a half to two hours, followed by two long breaks, but it's all based on crew coordination."

Delays have the biggest impact on a crew's duty day, which can be long, sometimes close to the maximum dictated by the Federal Aviation Administration. At Kalitta, the maximum is reduced in accordance with the pilot's union contract and for operational reasons two-hour extensions are permitted to keep the crew within maximum limits.

Describing typical flight durations, Chester said: "A lot of flights are one and done. We fly for eight hours and get off. There's also a fair number of flights that include a tech stop for picking up cargo. You may have two and a half hours scheduled on the ground which can drag out to three or four hours because the cargo has not arrived at the aircraft. Or with the cargo loaded you might have to wait for a push back crew, because we didn't catch them at the right time, so you can only wait. When that happens you start thinking about whether you have enough duty day left to fly? Do you need an extension? If you get an extension, do you still have enough time to fly?

"If it's a maintenance issue, the engineer and the maintenance department will decide if it is something you can defer and rectify later or if it's something that you need to fix immediately.

If the issue needs to be fixed immediately, how long is it going to take? If a deferral is sufficient, there are certain things that the engineer may have to do to the aeroplane for the deferral, and that takes time as well.

"During a snowstorm in Anchorage our flight was planned to go to Tokyo and then to Incheon. It was minus 17°F with a half a mile of visibility and moderate snow. You used a table loaded on an iPad to determine how long the de-icing fluid would last and we had to wait in line to be de-iced. Usually we de-ice on the spot, though some airports use a dedicated de-icing pad, which requires fuel to be burned to taxi. The de-icing truck had to fill up which took 30 minutes, so our wait time was an hour and a half given our position in the queue. This was a tech stop with no unloading or loading involved. We stopped at Anchorage to get fuel. We calculated the holdover time for the anti-ice fluid was to be about 20 minutes. Not long before the de-icing truck arrived, freezing fog was added to the weather report, further reducing the effectiveness of the anti-icing fluid to five minutes. The duty manager at our home station advised that the weather was forecast to improve within two hours and advised to wait and see what happened with the weather. As the de-icing process finished, freezing fog was dropped from the

weather forecast, at which point the decision was made to leave Anchorage bound for Ningbo, China. Watching the snowfall, you could see the green taxiway centreline lights getting slowly being obscured by the falling snow. After we departed Anchorage, the airport was closed to all the incoming traffic. The weather messed up schedules everywhere. Instead of a 20-hour layover in Korea, we were there for two and a half days waiting to come back and resume the schedule."

More recently, Chester flew from Incheon to Anchorage for a standard one-hour tech stop and then to New York-JFK. Describing the troublesome departure for JFK, he said: "A tyre needed to be changed which caused a delay that pushed us towards our maximum duty hour limit, so I requested extra fuel because the delay was likely to last a while. We eventually took-off and the flight to JFK was uneventful though the fuel burn seemed higher. Usually, you'd run ahead of your fuel state and not burn as much fuel as listed on the flight plan. It wasn't detrimental.

"Upon arrival to JFK, we were behind a Korean Airlines aircraft on the approach at 15 miles. Approach control broke us off and gave us an s-turn to build spacing on the Korean Airlines aircraft. We flew the approach at our minimal

> "Kalitta flies one route from Cincinnati to Incheon, South Korea. That's about 15 hours, so you've got to make sure that there's enough food on board and appropriate bedding for the bunks used by the crew for sleeping during en route rest periods."

approach speed. Based on fuel state, my concern was having to do a go around and sure enough, we did. When passing 500ft, an aircraft was still visible on the runway on its landing roll-out. Luckily, visibility was about 10 miles, so weather was not a concern, but the fuel state was. We landed with 16,000lb of fuel in the tanks, not much at all.

"Freight prices during the COVID pandemic went astronomical, probably double what they were pre-pandemic. We were flying in and out of China all the time. No one wanted to lay over in China and the Chinese didn't want anyone to lay over, but goods needed to be moved out. We made a night-stop at Incheon and flew for

up to four hours to destinations in China with a four-person crew. We then flew to Anchorage, so the crews were working a lot of long duty days. There were situations at Chinese airports when a maintenance issue caused a delay such that the crew had to stay on the aeroplane for 8, 10, 12 hours until a part could be flown in on a sister aircraft and the aircraft fixed. Chinese authorities would not allow the crew into the country because of the pandemic.

"Prior to a flight from Anchorage for Hong Kong, there was a problem with an air data computer, more specifically an altitude disagreement between the left and right sides. Computers were swapped. The flight had been

delayed a couple of hours for maintenance. On the climb out, an air date computer disagreement advisory popped up on the EFIS display meaning the left and right set of instruments didn't agree within the permitted limits. Discussions with a team based at headquarters led to the decision to continue with the flight and get rectification maintenance at Hong Kong. The aircraft might be placed in an AOG situation at Hong Kong and not be able to leave.

"Most 747s have three air data computers, so we went through a QRH [Quick Reference Handbook] procedure to isolate which one was wrong and run off the other two. Our jet had just two air data computers, only one of which was

serviceable. This meant the aircraft was no longer RVSM compliant and limited us to below 29,000ft altitude. We concluded we weren't going to make Hong Kong at the lower than planned altitude due to the increased fuel burn. After a further discussion with the company, this time with the duty officer, the recommendation was to return to Anchorage which was already close to weather minimums. I wanted to go to Seattle because we had an altimetry issue and the weather was much better there. The company pushed hard for Anchorage, it was doable, but we would need to dump fuel down to a safe landing weight. Nobody wants to take responsibility for dumping fuel. This caused a standoff. Is it okay to dump fuel? 'Well, captain do what you need to do'. Ok, I'm dumping fuel and returning to Anchorage. Once there they put us into rest while maintenance worked on the aircraft. The fault turned out to be a kink in one of the static lines, so they replaced the whole section, which probably meant the first air data computer was fine!"

CONFIGURATION IDIOSYNCRASIES

Kalitta Air operates a fleet of 22 Boeing 747 freighter aircraft, eight were converted from their original passenger configuration (747-400BCFs) and 14 were built as freighters on Boeing's then

> # "Watching the snowfall, you could see the green taxiway centreline lights getting slowly being obscured by the falling snow. After we departed Anchorage, the airport was closed to all the incoming traffic."

747 production line at Everett, Washington (747-400Fs). Five of the BCFs have GE engines, three have Pratt & Whitney engines. Of the factory freighters five have GE engines and nine have Pratt & Whitney engines. There's little difference between a BCF and a factory freighter, they operate and work the same, so all Kalitta air pilots fly both types with a Boeing 747-400 rating.

Discussing a couple of the aircraft's idiosyncrasies, Chester said: "Most of the aircraft do not have taxi lights, so the inboard landing lights are used instead. When originally ordered, the fixed taxi light that moves with the

nose gear was an option. Unlike a lot of other aeroplanes, the freighters are not equipped with a hot mic interphone system. So, when you want to talk to the other crew members through the communication system, you must use a mic switch. On any other aeroplane you have a voice activated switch to talk back and forth, so a lot of times, you're shouting back and forth such as when we're running our checklist on the ground. You talk out loud to make sure that everyone can hear what's going on, including the two pilots in the back, who depending on the setup, may not have a full audio panel."

Kalitta Air contracts to the US Air Force. Its Boeing 747s are seen at overseas bases including RAF Mildenhall, England where Boeing 747-446(BCF) N742CK is seen landing on December 10, 2018. Chris Wood

Flight Service Manager

Mal MacKinnon joined Virgin Atlantic in 1984 when the company had just one 747-200 classic and one route, Gatwick to Newark, New Jersey. Originally serving as a junior cabin crew, Mal has served as a flight services manager for 36 years.

Back in the summer of 1984, Mal MacKinnon had eight days of training on the 747 learning the emergency procedures and basic first aid taught to him by a former nurse working for Virgin Atlantic. The training concluded with an exam. Mal concedes that the training in 1984 was very different to today's six-week intensive training course and its requisite high pass mark. Whatever the differences to today, Mal passed his training which has served

him well throughout a 40-year tenure with Virgin Atlantic.

Cabin crew do annual recurrent training. Before the COVID-19 pandemic, Virgin introduced digital exams which cabin crew could do at home. They are timed to complete as many as 40 questions and must achieve an 80% pass mark. Commenting, Mal said: "Even though it's an open book exam, the nerves are still there because if you don't pass the exam, and you get two attempts, you must then go through a verbal examination, and if you don't pass that you're out the door."

Today, Mal is based at Manchester, flying on Virgin's Airbus A330-300 and A350-1000 aircraft,

but he cut his teeth on the mighty Boeing 747, both classics and 400s. He flew his first line flight from Gatwick to Newark in 1984 and his since flown every city pairing in Virgin's network.

FLIGHT SERVICE MANAGER
The editor spoke with Mal on the eve of a nine-hour, 30-minute flight from Manchester to Bridgetown, Barbados, a regular service operated by Virgin. We discussed the procedures required for flight from briefing to arrival at destination. Based on the A330 flight, but also applicable to the 747.

On flight day, Mal arrived at Manchester Airport two hours before the scheduled time

Mal MacKinnon (centre) in his first year of service with Virgin Atlantic. Virgin Atlantic/Mal MacKinnon

"We used to have 18 cabin crew on a 747 to cover each of its 12 doors and help evacuate up to 435 passengers in the event of an incident."

passenger load and the number of passengers in each class. Each cabin crew has an iPad and reiterates the information I've given them. I then allocate the cabin they'll be serving in and their working position in that cabin. "Then I'll hand the discussion to the CSS who will brief on how they would like things to run in the premium and economy cabins, in accordance with the company's set procedure. The CSS will also notify the cabin crew of passengers with mobility issues, those that use a wheelchair and which seat number they are in. After a team chat with loads of encouragement, the CSS then hands the discussion back to me. I'll then go through the standard lay down procedures and ask everybody a question to make sure that their knowledge of the aircraft type we're flying on, is up to scratch.

"The questions are generated on the day from a pool of questions held on the iPad. For example, 'can you tell me all the emergency equipment you have at your allocated door'? So, it's detailed and can put people on the spot. People get nervous, but in general, we're all there to make sure the knowledge is good so we can go on board and fly that aircraft safely."

Once the briefing is finished, the troupe go through staff security, get their bags checked and scanned and walk to the designated gate.

The aircraft should be ready for the crew to board when they arrive at the gate. The term 'turnaround 150' is used by Virgin to denote its one hour and 50-minute targeted time between the aircraft landing and taking off again. Explaining, Mal said: "This doesn't always happen, but the target from landing is to get all the passengers off, get the aircraft cleaned, de-catered, re-catered, new cabin crew and passengers on, doors closed and off, all within one hour and 50 minutes.

"Once on board, each individual cabin crew knows what they have to do at their assigned station. Primarily they run the relevant equipment checks, and report anything that's not quite right to the FSM who relays the issue via the captain to the engineers requesting they come on board to try and fix the issue. At that

of departure and met-up with nine other cabin crew and two pilots at the briefing rooms. Pilots use one room, cabin crew another.

The cabin crew comprises a flight service manager (FSM) who is in overall charge of the cabin crew and oversees everything within the cabin and is answerable only to the captain. The FSM title was once called the in-flight supervisor. The FSM is deputised by a cabin service supervisor (CSS), once called the purser, who works as a member of the cabin crew and predominantly supervises the economy and the premium cabins on board the aircraft. Both roles are classed as onboard managers. The remaining people are a mix of junior and senior cabin crew.

Mal said: "We used to have 18 cabin crew on a 747 to cover each of its 12 doors and help evacuate up to 435 passengers in the event of an incident. On an A330 we serve up to 285 passengers with ten cabin crew to

cover eight doors. Once, a 747-cabin crew included an inflight beautician, who did ladies nails and massages onboard the aircraft. The beautician was a member of the cabin crew and CAA certified on all the safety aspects of the 747.

As a flight service manager, Mal gave the cabin crew a standard pre-flight briefing which starts with a welcome and includes a check that everybody is fit to fly mentally, emotionally, and physically. This gives any member of the crew a chance to speak with Mal one-to-one if they're not feeling up to the flight, or if something's not right with them on the day.

Mal explained the rest of the briefing: "With everybody ready to go, I'll read through an overview of the flight that day. Starting with my own introduction, I also introduce the cabin service supervisor and go through all the basics, the aircraft type, expected

Mal MacKinnon on board a Virgin Atlantic Boeing 747. Virgin Atlantic/Mal MacKinnon

Mal MacKinnon and a colleague out on the ramp next to a Virgin Atlantic Airbus A330-300. Today Mal is a flight service manager with Virgin Atlantic. *Virgin Atlantic/Mal MacKinnon*

point the cabin crew must get everything ready in the cabin for the passengers and complete the emergency checks.

"While those procedures are underway, one cabin crew in the upper-class galley and the CSS in the lower galley check the catering to ensure we have enough meals to serve on the flight. My goal is to start passenger boarding 55 minutes before departure at which point, I notify the turnaround coordinator to allow the gate staff to start the boarding process. This took up to 40 minutes on a 747."

EN ROUTE SERVICE
Discussing the work performed by the cabin crew after take-off, Mal said: "The captain gives me the nod when the aircraft has passed 20,000ft such that the cabin crew can start the designated work. I make a PA announcement with the standard safety aspects and introduce the CSS to the economy and premium passengers and recommend they sit back and relax. Then the cabin crew start service in each cabin. From take-off it generally takes on average three hours to get the first service done. I then make sure that the cabin crew are given adequate rest to make the flight legal. For every six hours of work, they have 20 minutes to sit down for a cup of tea or coffee and something to eat. I split the breaks evenly, so the cabin is not unmanned. Two hours before landing we start the second service, which is usually an afternoon tea service.

"Once we land at our destination, 30 minutes later, the cabin crew is technically off duty but

> ## "The term 'turnaround 150' is used by Virgin to denote its one hour and 50-minute targeted time between the aircraft landing and taking off again."

of course we are responsible for ensuring all the passengers who use wheelchairs or need assistance safely get off the aircraft. Once all passengers have left the aircraft, we complete our post flight checks to ensure the safety equipment is back where it's meant to be and ready for the next crew. Then we walk off the aircraft and head to immigration, then collect our bags, make our way through customs and out to the bus for transportation to the hotel.

"On a one-night layover we generally have 24 hours rest. I make sure rooms are given to all the crew members as quickly as possible, quite

often using the hot-bed concept so the arriving crew occupy the rooms previously used by the departing crew, after cleaning of course. Crew need to go to their rooms as quickly as possible to avoid any effect on their next flight duty period. Some may choose to have a drink in the bar that evening, but nobody will go anywhere near alcohol on the day that we depart because it's a violation. We can be tested for alcohol and drugs at anytime, anywhere in the world, it's very stringent as it should be."

Discussing another aspect of the FSM's role Mal said: "Once the flight deck doors are closed, the pilots must have the confidence that everything or anything that could happen in the cabins will be taken care of by the FSM and cabin crew professionally and to the best of their abilities without having to bother them. That's my main role. For example, if a passenger is having a suspected heart attack, which can happen at any time, cabin crew attend to the person. We put out a request for a medically qualified person to volunteer to provide help. I speak with the captain, we do an assessment, we speak with a doctor from MedLink, who provides medical advice and assistance, based on the passenger's signs and symptoms. Between the doctor, the captain, and myself we decide if we're going to continue with the planned flight or divert to a nearby airport so the passenger can be admitted to hospital.

"My role in general, is to generate a happy working environment for the cabin crew and in conjunction with the flight deck crew get us to the destination as safely as we possibly can."

Cabin Crew and Turnaround Coordinator

Victoria Jones served as cabin crew and a turnaround coordinator with Virgin Atlantic. In this fascinating story she provides insight to the training required to become a cabin crew, some of the daily challenges of the job, and her role as an aircraft turnaround coordinator.

The captain of a Virgin Atlantic 747-400 taxies away from the ramp area after push-back following another on time dispatch. *Victoria Jones*

Victoria was prompted to apply for a cabin crew job by some members of a Virgin Atlantic cabin crew on a flight back from the United States. The conversation took place 35,000 feet over the United States and led Victoria to want to join Virgin Atlantic in particular, and to serve on the 747. She was working in a customer service role at the time she applied, and she had a big interest in hospitality and looking after people. What more could Virgin want!

After sending her application in to Virgin, she eventually received an invitation to an assessment day at the airline's flight centre in Crawley near Gatwick airport. Recalling the day, Victoria said: "While travelling to Crawley, I felt nervous but determined to do my best to get selected. The day comprised various exercises designed to determine a candidate's aptitude and abilities, two tests, one math, one English, and a two-on-one interview which was conducted in a somewhat relaxed environment. Later in my career with Virgin, I had responsibility for training both my interviewers. Three weeks later, I was offered a cabin crew job with Virgin which was considered at the time to be the golden egg job for cabin crew. I accepted the offer, moved to Brighton, and started the six-week training programme. This was divided into stages, one for the aircraft specific safety training which as cabin crew was a significant part of the training, a week of aviation medicine training, and finally cabin service training, learning about the procedures used and the products offered to passengers. We practiced serving food to each other in a cabin training rig. And we took an exam every day, so you really had to know the details. For the initial safety training we did wet dip drills in the pool, inflated life jackets, and pulled each other into a life raft, which is a pass or fail event, and people do fail that event and not get through the course, so you really had to be on your A game."

Despite Virgin's 747-centric fleet, Victoria was trained throughout the six weeks on the Airbus A330 and A340. She then did a five-day conversion course to learn about the aircraft she really wanted to serve

Victoria Jones served as a turnaround coordinator with Virgin Atlantic after completing her time as cabin crew. *Victoria Jones*

"For the initial safety training we did wet dip drills in the pool, inflated life jackets, and pulled each other into a life raft, which is a pass or fail event."

Job done. Victoria Jones smiling after dispatching a Boeing 747-400 aircraft on time to its destination. *Victoria Jones*

Victoria Jones smiles for the camera on the air stairs parked against a Virgin Atlantic Boeing 747. Victoria Jones

aboard, the 747. Commenting on the 747 course, Victoria said: "We were taught about the standard operating procedures, safety procedures, and the service we were required to provide. There was much more to learn compared to the A330 because the 747 had an upper deck."

HAIR, LIPSTICK, AND NAILS

Any reader who has had the good fortune to fly with Virgin Atlantic will surely not fail to remember the immaculacy of its cabin crew and the way in which the scarlet colour of the uniforms stands out in every airport. Such a level of presentation is achieved through training and regular appraisal. Explaining the background to Virgin cabin crew appearance, Victoria said: "Before you start your training, you visit a uniform team to get your uniform fitted and ready for training. During service training we received tuition of how to do our hair, make-up, and nails. We had to wear red lipstick, have red nails, and were taught what shade of red lipstick best suited our skin tone. A whole day was allocated to doing your hair, so no wispy bits, always slicked back, a bun or a French knot was preferable.

"You were marked on your grooming, and once in service, the flight's purser would also mark how you performed your job, how you were with the customers, and your standard of grooming throughout the flight, even at three o'clock in the morning. A testament to how cabin crew care about their appearance could be seen by the reaction to people stopping

and staring in the airport as an 18-person 747 crew, all looking immaculate walked by."

FIRST FLIGHT

Toward the end of her 747 training, Victoria and her fellow cabin crew received their

first work roster, delivered, as she recalls, in a brown A4 envelope. Discussing her first flight Victoria said: "Part of our training was a requirement to learn all the airport codes so that you knew where you were going. My first 747 flight was to Boston. I was excited

A busy ramp at London-Gatwick with four Virgin Atlantic 747s parked on the stands. Victoria said her time working as a turnaround coordinator with Virgin Atlantic was one of her favourite jobs. Victoria Jones

but so nervous because now I had to put everything learned into practice. Once on board the aircraft I just thought it was huge. My allocated supernumerary position was in the economy cabin where I was supervised by my purser doing my equipment checks. I almost forgot everything as I was so nervous! My mentor helped me with the check, she was phenomenal.

"Passenger boarding seemed never ending and trying to remember where everything was located was challenging because the aircraft was so big. The moment I realised that I was working on this iconic aircraft, was special."

That first flight to Boston, Massachusetts turned into a snowy, frozen event. What should have been a one-night trip ended up being four days. The flight arrived amidst one of the biggest snowstorms in East Coast history, a meteorological event known as the Blizzard of 2003. Recalling the experience, Victoria said: "As a rookie, I thought the crew were winding me up. On the day we were supposed to fly home, I went down to the hotel checkout anyway, but nobody was there, the crew had not been winding me up. Consequently, we had four frozen days in Boston. It's common for the crew to play a trick on the rookie. On the way home from Boston the purser asked me to take a drink to a passenger in row 82, they're angry so please go now was her instruction. I was looking everywhere for row 82, even upstairs, but I couldn't find it. They had me walking around for about half an hour trying to find row 82. No wonder, row 82 didn't exist on the 747.

"I also remember how tired I felt on the way home. I was doing the duty-free round which could take hours on the 747 because

you've got hundreds of people on board, not to mention the technical aspect to that job, and a bit of math to be done when adding up the purchases made by the passengers. I remember thinking it's three o'clock in the morning, what have I done, I'm so tired. That said, one of the great things about the 747 was

> *"Once in service, the flight's purser would also mark how you performed your job, how you were with the customers, and your standard of grooming throughout the flight, even at three o'clock in the morning."*

that you had a crew rest area with bunks where you could sleep for a bit of the journey. Thank goodness I was able to do that after the duty-free round was complete!"

MOVING ON UP

When Victoria joined Virgin Atlantic, all new cabin crew were rated as junior. Once promoted, based on their personal performance, they were rated as a cabin service supervisor after which they took a five-day course to learn about the products and service offered in upper class. That's a very coveted role for a cabin crew. Providing some insight, Victoria said: "We were taught about the different sort of clientele who travelled in upper-class and their expectations. Attention to detail was the primary requirement for cabin crew. Training included a visit to a London-based wine merchant that supplied Virgin to taste the wines to be served onboard. This enables a cabin crew to make an appropriate wine recommendation to a passenger. Cabin service supervisors were also trained to work in the galley preparing food for the other crew to serve to passengers as opposed to working from the aisle in a customer-facing role."

During her time serving as a cabin service supervisor Victoria had to deal with numerous incidents on board. On a return flight from Johannesburg, a young baby got sick and was unresponsive to any first aid care. Explaining the situation, Victoria said: "I was working up a rank as the flight service manager in charge of the cabin and remember conversations about the baby with the flight crew and specialist doctors working for MedLink who provide remote medical advice from their base in Arizona. Everybody was very concerned. At

An empty plane ahead of its next group of passengers was a familiar sight for Victoria when she served as a turnaround coordinator with Virgin Atlantic. Victoria Jones

> *"That first flight to Boston, Massachusetts turned into a snowy, frozen event. What should have been a one-night trip ended up being four days."*

able to continue to London where paramedics were waiting to take the baby straight to hospital. Sometimes the unwell passenger leaves the aircraft, and you don't receive a follow-up, but on this occasion, we later learned that the baby made a full recovery which was the news we all wanted to hear."

TURNAROUND COORDINATOR

When Victoria stopped flying full time with Virgin Atlantic, she didn't leave the company but moved into safety training as an instructor, a role that required her to learn the safety manuals for all aircraft types in Virgin's fleet. Explaining, Victoria said: "There are two types of training. Refresher training which occurs every 12 and 36 months and involved door drills and exams, and new hire training which involved teaching brand new people hired by the company. Unsurprisingly, most of the new people knew nothing about the airline industry or the 747. As an introduction, we used to take the new hire people on an aircraft tour so they could look at the equipment. Everybody was fascinated by the aircraft, its size, the upper deck, the crew rest area upstairs."

Following her tenure as a safety instructor, Victoria had an opportunity to move into airports training, a move that led to her becoming a turnaround coordinator (TCO) or dispatcher. It's a job that involves working on the ramp to receive and dispatch aircraft and managing all the requisite processes, for example, determining the aircraft's weight and balance through the load sheet, and getting the fuel payload figure from the pilot.

Victoria described the TCO as an exciting role at the heart of the operation: "Effectively, you're the controller of all above wing and below wing activities, and your main job is to get that aircraft away safely and on time or a few minutes early if possible. You coordinate everything. Is everybody checked in? Is everybody at the gate? How much baggage is to be loaded? Sometimes a bag could be flagged for which you needed to get the passenger that owned the bag to open it on the ramp. You work very closely with the loading team and the loading supervisor to ensure that everything listed on the documentation and

the time we were flying over central Africa, a location that offered few airports we could reach quickly. As the flight service manager all my decisions for the cabin were influenced by the wellbeing and safety of passengers and crew, whilst working closely with the captain who looks after the security situation of potential diversion airports. There are always so many decisions that must be made to divert an aircraft whatever the location. For me it was a standout career moment because despite the challenges presented and the learning curves experienced it showed how good the team was with the help of some medically qualified passengers when needed.

"The priority is of course the unwell passenger, and thank goodness the baby started to come around just as the flight crew were preparing to divert. It was a hairpin decision, because if we had diverted all the crew would have been out of duty hours. That would have meant waiting for their statute rest time to elapse before we could have continued the flight back to London. Given the baby's improving condition, the flight was

manifest are getting loaded and in the correct locations. You have responsibility for safety on the ramp ensuring there is nothing on the ramp that should not be there and that nobody parked a vehicle in a no parking zone.

"For me, the hardest thing was moving the jetty or air bridge up to or from the aircraft partly because you knew everybody onboard the aircraft was desperate to get underway or disembark. So, the pressure of putting the jetty in position was always accompanied with an element of what if I damage the multimillion-pound aircraft, and what if I dented it? Thankfully, that never happened as we were so well trained and you held a separate licence to operate the jetty, but I was always a little nervous!"

Working at Gatwick, Victoria and her colleagues worked from a facility within a hub called The Gatehouse where the entire crew checked in. This allowed the TCO to speak with

On its way to the runway at London-Gatwick Airport, Virgin Atlantic Airways' Boeing 747-443 G-VROY Pretty Woman. Chris Wood

Virgin Atlantic Airways' Boeing 747-4Q8 G-VFAB Lady Penelope *on push-back from the stand at London-Gatwick Airport. Chris Wood*

the crew and give them any special information related to the flight including the cargo, any dangerous goods, and animals on board the aircraft, and to complete a cross check of all documentation. The TCO would also speak to the flight service manager about boarding time expectations and various other elements of the pre-departure procedures. Discussing the process, Victoria said: "The aircraft absolutely cannot go unless everything is cross checked, and triple checked with regards to the passengers onboard being in the right zone and that all baggage is correct and accounted for. You work closely with the flight crew, the cabin crew, the ground teams, and the ground supervisor assigned to your flight, who notify you when a passenger arrives late to check in and whether they can be accepted to board the aircraft. That's the TCO's decision. Will the aircraft be delayed, and can we get their bag loaded in time? Similarly,

if all baggage is onboard but we are missing a passenger, do I offload the bags, or do we wait?

"There's a lot of moving pieces to the TCO role and it is stressful. One difficulty with every flight was trying to get to the 747's flight deck to speak with the captain about any issues during boarding. Why? Because it's at the top of the stairs, at the very front of the aircraft, and proves tricky to reach during boarding with lots of people around. But it was a very exciting role and when you got a 747 away on time it was always a satisfying feeling. But everybody played their part in getting that aircraft away on time. From the pilot's perspective, they were busy, but if they hadn't sent their check list figures on time, you had to give them a gentle nudge to complete that task otherwise the load sheet would be delayed, which would in turn delay departure."

Ever the determined, Victoria relinquished her TCO role to become a cabin crew manager based

at Gatwick. The TCO role was one that requires a licence and to remain current to complete a set number of turnarounds per month. Victoria, with her manager's blessing, was able to keep her well-earned licence and for a period of her cabin crew manager tenure she was still able to dispatch an aircraft. In her new manager role, there were times where she was able to switch hats during periods of operational need, when she could go down to the ramp and meet or dispatch the aircraft as well as fulfilling her cabin crew manager position.

Summing up, Victoria said: "I loved the TCO role, it was one of my favourite jobs. Dispatching an A330 was not the same as a 747, because it was just iconic. Having worked on all the aircraft types operated by Virgin, either on the ground or in training, it was always the aircraft that people wanted to talk about."

Loadmaster

Ron Lambert started out working on the ramp at Ypsilanti Willow Run Airport then trained as a load specialist on DC-9s before joining Kalitta Air for a three-week Boeing 747 loadmaster training course.

Loading of pallets off a K-loader onto a Kalitta Air Boeing 747. US Air Force/Senior Airman Zachary Cacicia

Loadmasters working for Kalitta Air are all home based and use a domicile airport from where they fly to a destination where their 747 aircraft is located.

Ron's training comprised two weeks in the classroom working ten-hour days, learning the company's ramp operations manual and hazardous material training. He then spent a week at Kalitta's maintenance base in Oscoda, Michigan, doing hands on training, for example learning strapping plans.

Used to working with USA Jet Airlines' relatively small DC9s which measure just over 100ft in length, the first thing Ron realised about working with the Boeing 747 was the size of the aircraft and the responsibility he was to take when operating the monster. Recalling when he learned from the manual, Ron said: "The standout aspects were the amount of cargo that could fit in the 747, the size of the equipment and pallets of cargo it could hold, and its weight limit. The max gross take-off weight of a DC-9

was 90,000lb, with a 747-400 the max gross take-off weight was 873,000lb. Learning the floor loading limits, and lateral limits, taught me the huge numbers I was having to deal with. Only one thing needs to go wrong, and the aircraft's safety of flight is put in jeopardy.

"The first week of classroom training was dedicated to the ramp ops manual with an examination that consisted of about 100 questions. That's a big test. It took me about

seven and a half hours to get through the test. It was open book but finding everything in the manual took time with more time spent on answering each question.

During the second week, we were taught about the types of hazardous materials that Kalitta carries and the dangers of flying such materials. For example, lithium-ion batteries, which concern everyone in the industry because they're so volatile. Whenever we

carry hazardous materials, we must fill out a NOTOC [notice to the captain] form that labels every type of hazardous material on board. The NOTOC is given to the captain and forwarded to various departments in the company. If there's ever an in-flight emergency, and we divert, that information can be passed on to local officials at the diversion field, so they can deal with the situation accordingly once we land."

The International Federation of Air Line Pilots' association (IFALP) list the NOTOC as:

"The sole regulatory source of information provided to the flight crew as to the nature and quantity of the dangerous goods carried as cargo and serves to assess the severity of an inflight incident."

Ron continued: "Week three [of the training] was spent at Oscoda, learning how to operate a 747's cargo doors, familiarising with the layout of the floors in the aeroplane, learning how to load different types of cargo, creating strapping plans, and doing chain-to-pallet and strap-to-pallet exercises to learn how

A Kalitta Air loadmaster reads the load plan while standing next to the wall-mounted control panel as cargo is loaded onto a Kalitta Air Boeing 747. US Air Force/Senior Airman Zachary Cacicia

to properly secure cargo in the plane. We worked on a retired 747 classic and followed the instructions given by our instructor. For example, 'centre load this 20ft sea container on the floor'. The instructor handed us a strapping plan, we picked some straps and strapped the container down according to that strapping plan. The facility has an old aircraft engine. The instructor told us its weight and asked us to load it by putting straps on it, checking the angles of the straps, and making sure the right amount of restraint is applied for the floor position on the aircraft.

"Once the aircraft engine was strapped down, we used a protractor app on our phones to check the strap angles, the floor angle, and the centreline angle. Then we entered the details into a spreadsheet which calculated the amount of restraint a strap was providing

Cargo pallets are loaded into a Kalitta Air Boeing 747 freighter. US Air Force/Senior Airman Zachary Cacicia

"The first thing Ron realised about working with the Boeing 747 was the size of the aircraft and the responsibility he was to take when operating the monster."

whether for forward or aft strength or lateral left and right restraint. Post-check if the straps did not meet requirements, we added more straps at different angles and measured out the connection points to ensure there was 20 inches between them. Whatever the strapping plan, our own or one that's already engineered for that specific type of cargo, the loadmaster had to measure out all the connection points. All straps are the same. We don't typically use a ratchet style strap to pull the slack out and bind it in. Each strap is 45mm wide, the same length [seven, nine, or 13 metres], and rated to a breaking load of 5,000lb. Each aircraft carries a lot of straps on board.

"At the end of the three-weeks of training we were awarded a company certificate. Each year, we do recurrent training which is all computer-based with different testing

modules. Then we complete practical worksheets, a load plan, and practice strapping a pallet, all to keep us proficient because there are some procedures that a loadmaster might not perform for a whole year."

Explaining the loadmaster role, Ron said: "Responsibilities of a loadmaster start at the cargo door where the main cargo panel is located. Ground handlers help us to load. As pallets are pushed on board the aircraft, I use my load plan to verify the pallet ID, the weight, and its destination. We also check the integrity of the nets over the cargo to make sure they meet the requisite standards. There are limits to the amount of damage to a net which is what we inspect them for. Loading is a fast-paced operation because sometimes we might have a short amount of time on the ground, we need to offload and re-load in two hours.

"A load plan takes care of the way that the load is distributed and secured and the location of each ULD (unit load device which is a pallet or a container) on the jet, and how they are loaded into an aircraft.

"Usually, the cargo terminal operator will send the handler a dead load weight statement giving details of all cargo booked on the flight.

The handler arranges the pallets and containers in the order they need to be loaded on the aircraft and references each pallet's ID number. Sometimes pallets and containers arrive out of sequence. Depending on the time available, it's okay to accept a palette or container out of sequence, because I can use my weight and balance programme to move the pallets around

and that should keep the aircraft centre of gravity within the operating envelope. The most I've ever received out of sequence is three.

"Some pallets have height restrictions, especially those to be positioned close to the aircraft's nose under the crew deck where the limit is 96 inches. Every floor position has a contour, which is always important, especially

A turbofan aircraft engine carried in a steel frame strapped to the floor of a Kalitta Air Boeing 747 freighter. *Kalitta Air/Ron Lambert*

if the pallet is built tall. Pallets can be built up to 118in high to fit on the main deck. As each pallet comes onto the aircraft, we make sure it's not contacting the ceiling or the sidewall. As loadmaster, I must know the restrictions for all floor positions of the aircraft.

"All pallets and containers must be loaded to a maximum gross weight to avoid eccentricity

in load concentration on the deck. We want to spread the load around the pallet and depending on what's loaded on the pallet, if it's centralised, you want to make sure it's shored out to spread the weight evenly.

"The only time we use chains is for a military flight to provide additional strength for a particular load, but chains add a lot more

weight. Depending on how many chains we use, their collective weight can add hundreds of pounds to a pallet."

MILITARY FLIGHTS

Kalitta Air operates lots of flights on contract to the US Air Force. This usually requires the aircraft to land at a base to collect the cargo. Explaining

The nose loading door rotates upward to enable pallets and containers to be loaded on board a 747 freighter. *Kalitta Air/Ron Lambert*

The gargantuan cargo cabin of a Kalitta Air Boeing 747 freighter aircraft. *Kalitta Air/Ron Lambert*

> "The only time we use chains is for a military flight to provide additional strength for a particular load, but chains add a lot more weight... their collective weight can add hundreds of pounds to a pallet."

the process, Ron said: "I try to arrive at the air base at least three hours prior to the aircraft's arrival and will inspect the cargo if I have the opportunity, which saves having to inspect the cargo as it's getting loaded. Once I'm onboard the aircraft I put all the floor pallet locks down, they are up when the aircraft is empty. I'll receive an AF Form 4080 on an Excel spreadsheet, copy, and paste the information into an internet-based weight and balance programme called CHAMP and save the information in the system. I can access the information from any computer. Then I create a load plan. The air force handlers will deliver the cargo to the aircraft in the order listed on its 4080 form which is the same as the CHAMP load plan. They are in different formats."

Known as a load sequence breakdown worksheet, the AF Form 4080 provides a detailed breakdown of the sequence in which cargo and equipment are loaded onto an aircraft. The form documents details of various loads being carried by the aircraft, including their weight, dimensions, and placement within the cargo hold, pallet IDs, destinations and whether it's hazardous material or not. This information helps the load crew and loadmaster to effectively manage and distribute cargo to maintain optimal balance and safety during flight.

Discussing the hands-on work at the aircraft, Ron said: "We start loading the aircraft as quickly and safely as possible. Concurrently, I'll coordinate with the flight mechanic to get the aircraft refuelled. As each pallet or container is transferred to its position, it is locked in place with restraint equipment. If we have any locks that are inoperative or missing, you take a penalty on the restraint or on the weight of the cargo so we must pay attention to any such issue.

"The floor of the main deck is fitted with wheels called pallet drive units [PDUs] which are operated by switches on the wall-mounted control panel located near the main cargo door. Each pallet or container is transferred from the K-loader onto the actual deck of the aircraft, and you can then drive that item to the place it needs to be with the PDU in operation. The PDUs are rotated back and forth, left, and right, using the joystick controller. Should the PDUs not work, loading is very difficult.

"Learning how to load a 20ft pallet took me some time. The pallet is loaded long ways, 20ft from left to right, then you must spin it in the door to be able to run it along the side of the plane. Unless the loadmaster is watchful of how the pallet comes in the door, it may be built up a certain way, and moves until the contours are correct, it could collide with the inside of the aeroplane.

"Once all the cargo is loaded and properly secured in the position, I go back upstairs and enter the fuel numbers into the flight plan and CHAMP, the weight and balance programme, and send the information via ACARS to the cockpit for the captain. Then I walk around the aircraft to make sure all the doors are closed and secured, make sure there's no

damage to the aircraft from the loading process, and then give a loadmaster briefing to the captain before departure. Once that's complete, I close out the flight on CHAMP, at which point my pre-flight work is done.

"You generally work with a US Air Force Air Mobility Squadron whose load crew personnel bring me the paperwork to the aircraft and manifest the actual loading. Military personnel are only permitted to do so much on the aircraft because of their standards and regulations and rules, because they don't want to be held liable for certain things. Air Force personnel may help me load, but as far as operating the floor, their rules are set such that they're not allowed to operate the floor, so the mechanic may have to help me."

Kalitta flies a lot of commercial cargo into China, a process that follows broadly the same procedures as military cargo. Ron explained: "If I'm at Anchorage during my 20-day rotation waiting for an aircraft to arrive for the onward flight to a Chinese city, it's my responsibility to keep track of the plane en route to Anchorage. Using flight tracking software, once I see the plane, I'll contact the captain to verify the hotel pickup time for the shuttle that takes us to the aircraft. Usually, we don't make changes to cargo at Anchorage, it's a case of getting on the plane and leaving so I must update our manuals and our weight and balance programme and do my load master briefing. By the time we land at the Chinese airport, our ground

services department has already done our load plan. I check it and print it off, offload the cargo, reload the new cargo, do my trip report keeping track of all the start and finish times for every function of the operation on the ground, do the weight and balance and prepare for tale-off then back to Anchorage. I clear customs, return to the hotel, and wait for my next trip assignment. An example of a typical rotation involves me flying from Cincinnati to Anchorage, Anchorage to China, China to Incheon in South Korea, then back to Anchorage and I repeat that cycle for the rest of the 20 days. Loadmasters do not fall under any crew rest rules, like the pilots do. Loadmasters can get plenty of sleep while on board. We have two bunks for the resting pilots and two bunks for the mechanic and loadmaster."

BIG CHALLENGES

Kalitta Air's slogan is 'on time, anywhere, anytime', so for Ron, the biggest thing that weighs on his mind is being late. He said: "I always shoot for an on-time departure. Certain situations are out of my control, but I do everything in my power to keep everything rolling as smoothly as possible and be as on-time as is possible. I've arrived at the aircraft on time on many occasions and you might wait two hours for the cargo to show up to the plane. I've shown up for military flights only to be informed the cargo is not going to be ready for another 12 hours.

"In any such situation, the loadmaster keeps the aircraft captain informed about when the loading starts and its expected duration, especially if we're running tight on time, when the loading is done, and the final cargo weight. The flight plan is built partly off the expected payload. We're allowed to be within 10,000lb above or below the specified payload entered on the flight plan. If we exceed the 10,000lb margin a new flight plan is required based on the revised fuel burn rate.

"We have one extended range freighter in our fleet with a higher payload capability and a max gross weight take-off of 910,000lb. I've taken off in that plane at 909,000lb, but it can fly the same distance as a regular freighter."

Two Boeing 747-400s undergoing hangar maintenance. *British Airways*

Maintaining the Jumbo

Paul Robinson worked for several major airlines as a Civil Aviation Authority licenced engineer. Boeing 707s, BAC 1-11s, and McDonnell Douglas DC-10s kept him busy in his early years, but the greatest proportion of his work was maintaining the Boeing 747. Paul recollected some of his more notable experiences to the editor.

"Initially Paul Robinson worked on 747 classics which he recalled soaking up much more manpower time compared to the Boeing 707 and the BAC 1-11."

British Airways' mechanics perform maintenance on a Rolls-Royce RB211-524 turbofan engine, the chosen powerplant of the carrier's Boeing 747-400 fleet. *British Airways*

British Airways' mechanics fit a new wheel and tyre on one of the carrier's Boeing 747-400 fleet. *British Airways*

British Airways' mechanics work on the underfloor of a Boeing 747-400 during a major check. *British Airways*

Paul Robinson trained on the Boeing 747 at British Caledonian Airways' Gatwick training school. While there he spent five weeks learning about the 747's airframe and a further two weeks learning about the engine.

At the time, British Caledonian had two hangars at Gatwick which is where Paul first started maintaining the company's 747-200 aircraft. Explaining the set-up, he said: "The hangars were not big enough to park the whole aircraft. The aircraft's tail extended out of the front of the hangar, so we used a weatherproof tail dock to enclose the aircraft's tail. When we wanted to open the hangar to get the aircraft out, the tail dock was problematic, especially on a windy day. The dock was moved up and down on a set of rails powered by electro-hydraulic motors, when the dock was open it caught a lot of wind and acted like a big sail."

Initially Paul Robinson worked on 747 classics which he recalled soaking up much more manpower time compared to the Boeing 707 and the BAC 1-11. Discussing the types of work undertaken, he said: "Airframe wise, there were no major problems apart from the size of components like the landing gear actuators, how high they were off the ground, and their weight.

British Airways' mechanics re-position some steps to gain access to a point on the engine pylon. *British Airways*

Work platforms positioned around a Boeing 747-400 aircraft for a major check. Mechanics are working on the aircraft's wing leading edge devices. *Key Collection*

> **"The [Pratt & Whitney] JT9 was crude by design but tough, they could take a licking and keep on ticking."**

would very likely surge at some point in the test. From experience you could tell the engine was about to surge by the change in the intake note so you could throttle back and hopefully catch it before it surged. If a JT9 engine did surge, you'd throttle back and then start the check again by increasing the throttles to the required power setting and carry on. By comparison, if you had a CF6 or an RB211 engine surge during a maintenance engine run, you'd probably have to do borescope inspection of the compressor before continuing the engine run. That was because the CF6 and RB211 engines were more refined than the JT9, and less likely to surge, but if they did it generally meant an engine change.

"To perform a maintenance engine run, you sat in the captain's seat and used the throttles with another qualified engineer sat at the flight engineer's panel. You set the parking brake which would hold the aircraft without any problem, but for a just-in-case situation, we had somebody in the co-pilot's seat ready to stand on the brakes. We also had another engineer on the ramp wearing a headset to let us know if anything started moving. You performed a maintenance engine run if you had to change or test a variety of engine components such as a fuel control unit or a compressor control bleed system component, and of course for a complete engine change. You'd take the engine up to what we called part power setting, which is a very high-power setting, record all the parameters and check they're all within specified limits."

When the editor asked Paul if the JT9 was easier to work on than the CF6 and RB211, he replied: "Yes and no. You could get the side cowlings off a JT9 although they were a devil to put back on because they were so big and heavy. With the CF6, if you needed to get to the core of the engine you had to work under the thrust reverser cowling which opened outward. With the RB211 you had to take the panels off inside the thrust reverser c-duct and work in that area. On the CF6 and RB211, the engine

The 747's leading edge devices were normally operated by pneumatic power or by electrically powered motors as an alternative deployment method. In the maintenance environment, if you had the leading-edge devices deployed, you had to be very careful if you had to switch on the pneumatics for a totally different function because the leading-edge devices were set to operate pneumatically and would close within seven seconds. If there was anybody working up on the wing near the leading edges, they stood no chance. So, you had to be very mindful when you were in the cockpit flicking switches and firing up APUs."

Describing the 747's engines, Paul said: "The first engine type fitted to the 747 was the Pratt & Whitney JT9 which was like an agricultural engine compared to the General Electric CF6 and the Rolls-Royce RB211. The JT9 was crude by design but tough, they could take a licking and keep on ticking.

"In the early days of 747 operations, the inaugural Pam Am 747 flight from New York to Heathrow was delayed for several hours due to an engine change. After a short amount of time, the JT9 engine casing started to distort from circular

to an oval shape. As you can imagine, it's not very good for the turbine blades or compressor blades. The problem was fixed by fitting a yoke between the compressor casing and the rear mount to stop it distorting.

"During a maintenance engine run at high power if a JT9 encountered a cross wind it

China Airlines' Boeing 747-400 B-18210 is gradually towed into the maintenance dock of a large hangar. *Boeing Dreamscape/Wikimedia Commons*

gearbox was attached to the fan case and most of the components such as the fuel control unit and generator were attached to that, so you'd open the c-duct for access at head height. On a JT9, some of the components, like the bleed control system for the compressor control, were under the forward part of the engine under a diaphragm behind the fan. It was difficult to get at, I got stuck on one occasion while trying to stick a rigging pin into the bleed control unit. This meant reaching inside the diaphragm. My arm got stuck and I couldn't get out without a lot of wriggling and movement. Not only that, but the JT9 leaked at lot of oil, so everything was covered in oil meaning you got covered in oil.

"The JT9 had seven compressor-controlled bleed valves that were open and closed during the various engine power settings from start to idle to high power. Three of the bleed valves took air loads off the compressor during initial engine start and when she got to about 50%, they shut, leaving two of the main bleed valves open which would close as power increased. The bleed valve system sometimes caused problems. When the pilot throttled back to begin descent, the engine tended to surge which was generally caused by a bleed system fault. During high-power maintenance engine runs we could place indicator flags in the bleed valve exhausts and monitored when the valves opened and closed, by whether the flag stuck out against the fan exhaust air stream or was blown flat against the cowling which helped determine what the problem was.

"While working for a major airline, the company undertook its Civil Aviation Authority

Access to points on the aircraft that are high above the hangar floor are a challenge for engineers and mechanics working on a Boeing 747 aircraft. AirTeamImages/Edwin Chai

licencing flight with a 747 flying from Gatwick to Maastricht. As the aircraft rotated, air traffic controllers in Gatwick tower reported momentary flames coming out of the number two jet pipe. Once the aircraft got to steady state cruise the flight crew and ground engineer on board the aircraft used to the flight deck instruments to check all the engine parameters. They found nothing out of line. They carried on. At Maastricht, the engineers carried out

inspections of the front and back of the number two engine with no damage noted. The aircraft returned to Gatwick without any problems. Back in the hangar, we carried out a borescope inspection of the number two engine and found that the eight-stage compressor was devoid of all its blades. The compressor stage had failed, and all the blades went out the back of the engine proving that the JT9 could take a licking and carry-on ticking."

The stripped-down flight deck of a Boeing 747-400 during a major check. Dmitry Avdeev/Wikimedia Commons

The C-check interval on a Boeing 747-200 was 3,600 hours or 15 months, whichever came first. AirTeamImages/Bram Botterman

JT9D

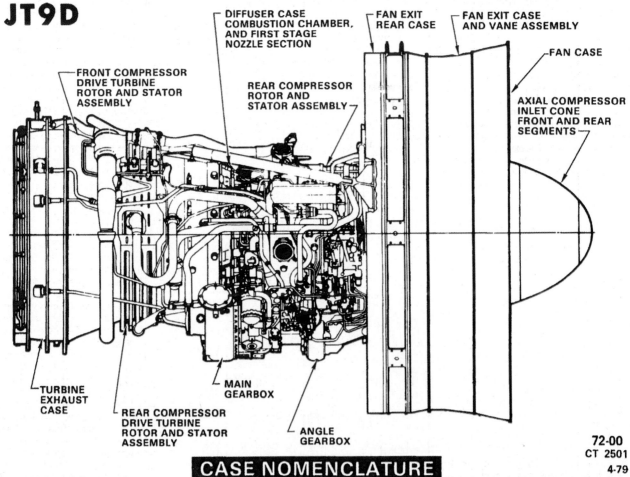

DIFFUSER CASE
COMBUSTION CHAMBER,
AND FIRST STAGE
NOZZLE SECTION

FAN EXIT
REAR CASE

FAN EXIT CASE
AND VANE ASSEMBLY

FAN CASE

FRONT COMPRESSOR
DRIVE TURBINE
ROTOR AND STATOR
ASSEMBLY

REAR COMPRESSOR
ROTOR AND
STATOR ASSEMBLY

AXIAL COMPRESSOR
INLET CONE
FRONT AND REAR
SEGMENTS

TURBINE
EXHAUST
CASE

REAR COMPRESSOR
DRIVE TURBINE
ROTOR AND STATOR
ASSEMBLY

MAIN
GEARBOX

ANGLE
GEARBOX

72-00
CT 2501
4-79

CASE NOMENCLATURE

A line drawing of a General Electric JT9D engine at side elevation. Pratt & Whitney via Paul Robinson

FOR TRAINING
PURPOSES ONLY

On another occasion while trouble shooting an engine surge defect, Paul had to boroscope the engine. To do that the air duct to the starter motor and starter valve had to be removed. On removing the duct several compressor blades fell out! Paul needed to go any further, it was an engine change.

Paul found a similar defect on a JT9 engine. "The aircraft was EGT-limiting [exhaust gas temperature] during take-off from Miami. When we performed a borescope of the engine, the eight-stage compressor blades were missing but there were no other issues. There's a maximum EGT limit for all power settings. At a hot location like Miami, you get close to the EGT limit. On take-off from Miami this particular engine was nearing the EGT limit, so the flight engineer throttled back the engine to keep it within the limits. EGT limiting is indicative of a fault with the engine or the engine getting old and tired which you would normally pick up in the condition monitoring data. With a 200 series aircraft, once in cruise on every flight, the flight engineer would record all the parameters, N1 [fan speed], N2 [HP compressor speed], EGT, fuel flow, vibration levels, configuration and so on. By plotting the data onto a graph, you could see if any parameter stepped out of line. Then you started investigating that problem and that's how engine condition monitoring was carried out. Both incidents resulted in an unscheduled engine change, but they weren't overly affecting the engine's performance."

FOUR HUNDRED

Discussing the changes brought about by the introduction of the Boeing 747-400, Paul said: "As 747-200s got older they became less reliable, particularly with components positioned on the aircraft located in harsh environments. For example, we got a lot of problems with brittle wiring to the wing leading edge temperature sensors that monitored for bleed leaks from the bleed ducts in the wing. The bleed ducts started to leak when the seals started to deteriorate. Issues associated with 747-200 classics were lost when the aircraft were retired and replaced by the 747-400 model, which

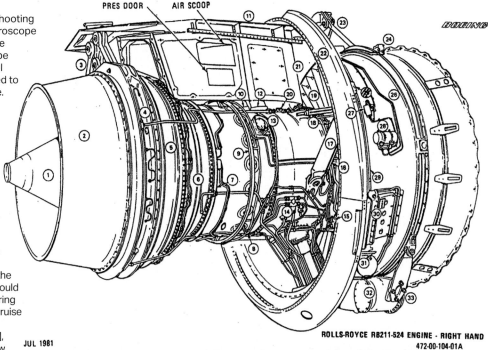

JUL 1981

ROLLS-ROYCE RB211-524 ENGINE - RIGHT HAND
472-00-104-01A

A line drawing of a Rolls-Royce RB211-524 engine from a right-side perspective. Rolls-Royce via Paul Robinson

from a ground engineer's perspective had the benefit of an aircraft condition monitoring system, which was much more capable than any system on a classic aircraft."

Paul continued: "We could get real time data off the aircraft at any time during the flight, it was also automatically transmitted. If the pilot wrote-up a hard landing or slight overspeed with the flaps extended, we could download the relevant parameters associated with the pilot's write up: altitude and Mach number for an overspeed or the airspeed and vertical descent rate for a hard landing. This gave us all the right information to carry out the right checks. The maintenance checking procedures followed a graduated methodology, so if you found no damage in section A you didn't have to bother with sections

B and C. However, if damage was found in section A you then had to look at the parameters for section B, and if that was free of damage you could ignore the section C checks.

"Another difference with the 400 was its carbon brake system which replaced the steel brakes used by the 747 classic. The 400's brake system had torque limiters which measured the amount of torque the brake was generating as the brakes were applied, and would then limit the amount of retardation because the brakes were that good. If the braking was unrestricted the braking action and resultant braking force could damage the landing gear struts. When the 400 first entered service, pilots were using the thrust reverser and brakes as they had on a 747 classic. Consequently, we found higher than expected brake wear. The brake manufacturer, BF Goodrich, advised us that carbon brakes operated at maximum efficiency in a certain temperature range with minimum wear. Deploying the thrust reversers took lots of energy out of the system so the brakes were never getting up to the optimum temperature, which increased the amount of brake wear. The company issued revised procedures which specified on landing the reversers were to be deployed to reverse idle only and the brakes be used to the maximum extent, i.e., to do all the work, and to only use the thrust reversers if necessary. Applying the new procedure not only saved the company a lot of money by reducing the amount of brake wear but also help maximise the life of the engine thrust reversers.

"Cabin temperature when the aircraft was on the ground at a hot location was also a problem with the 400." Explaining, Paul said: "During a turnaround in a hot location like Las Vegas the cabin got unbearably hot such that the APU-powered air conditioning system could not cool the temperature sufficiently for passengers boarding the aircraft. We carried out an investigation and eventually got the situation under control by mentoring the cabin crew to close all the cabin shades

ROLLS-ROYCE RB211-524 ENGINE - LEFT HAND
472-00-103-01A

A line drawing of a Rolls-Royce RB211-524 engine from a left side perspective. Rolls-Royce via Paul Robinson

after passengers had left the aircraft, the cargo doors were closed once unloading was complete, and the company ensured a big powerful ground air conditioning unit was available at the aircraft stand. We also enhanced our bleed air system leak checks. Boeing had dropped the requirements from its 747-maintenance programme which most airlines followed, but we ended up paying a price with unbearably hot cabin temperatures, so we reinstated the leak checks and got the benefit."

AIRBORNE EMERGENCY

During a flight from Gatwick to a North American destination, Paul got a call informing him a 747 aircraft had lost hydraulic fluid. Paul was aware of what maintenance had been carried out to the aircraft the night before and thought the loss of hydraulic fluid was related to the actuator that had been changed during that episode. The aircraft's captain reported loss of the hydraulic fluid during gear retraction which confirmed Paul's suspicions. When the aircraft was over the Bristol Channel, he advised the captain to return to Gatwick. Speaking about the incident, Paul said: "At that point we all thought it was a simple hydraulic leak, but when we saw the aircraft on the approach from the office, we noticed the aircraft wasn't descending but flying level. We called the tower to be told that the captain couldn't get the right-hand main wing landing gear down. The captain flew to an area off the south coast and flew in a circular pattern to try and shake the landing gear loose. While that was going on, a plane spotter called us to say he'd taken some photographs of the aircraft which he sent to us. His photos clearly showed that the wing landing gear was stuck on the landing gear door. Normally, if you perform a landing gear free fall because, for example, you have a hydraulic system problem, the up locks break and the three tonnes of gear comes down being damped by the remaining fluid in the actuator. On this occasion all the hydraulic fluid in the actuator was lost, there was nothing to dampen the landing gear and it fell out like a dead weight.

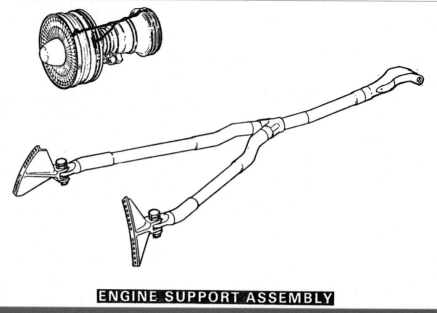

ENGINE SUPPORT ASSEMBLY

During the early days of JT9D operations on Boeing 747s, the engine casing distorted from circular to an oval shape, causing damage to turbine and compressor blades. The problem was fixed by fitting a yoke to the casing to prevent distortion. A line drawing of a yoke or engine support assembly fitted to Pratt & Whitney JT9D engines.

"Landing gear doors have a striker plate. In freefall, one of the tires contacts the striker plate which pushes the door the rest of the way open. Because the main leg fell out undamped, it hit the striker plate, which snapped it off and because the door wasn't pushed out of the way, the landing gear caught on the door, and there was no way it was coming down. Fortunately, the 747 is designed to land on two main landing gears, so with three operable a landing was possible. Because it was late December, we wanted to get the aircraft on the ground in daylight. When the aircraft touched down on the runway, the right-wing landing gear was stuck on the landing gear door, but the aircraft came to a stop on the runway with the right wing down.

"It was subsequently determined that the hydraulic retract actuator on the right-wing landing gear actuator was installed 180° out of alignment, effectively it was installed upside down. During the landing gear retraction, a linkage swings down, but because the actuator was upside down, the linkage knocked one of fittings off the actuator, which was the leak point from where the hydraulic fluid was lost. Consequently, the company wrote its own technical bulletin setting out the requirement for a gear swing when a landing gear actuator was changed which was not required in the Boeing maintenance manual. Several major airlines experienced the same situation."

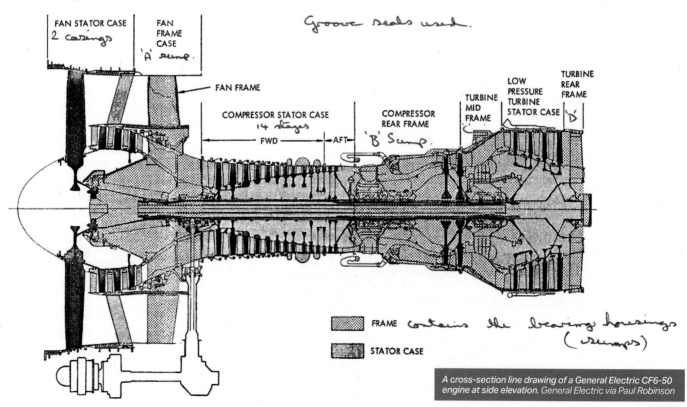

A cross-section line drawing of a General Electric CF6-50 engine at side elevation. General Electric via Paul Robinson

Kalitta Air

Apprentice

Located at Oscoda-Wurtsmith Airport, Michigan, Kalitta Air Maintenance is responsible for servicing the company's fleet of Boeing 747 freighter aircraft. Part of the maintenance operation at the site is the Kalitta Air Maintenance Training facility. According to the company it combines multiple classrooms with full media support, labs for practical training exercises, computer-based training stations and on-site Federal Aviation Administration testing.

The centre is run by the maintenance training department which ensures that airline employees are properly trained to perform their assigned job functions with the requisite technical proficiency. Staff provide instructor-led and computer-based training aircraft maintenance including a 30-month apprenticeship programme focussed on qualifying an apprentice with an FAA Airframe and Powerplant Mechanic (A&P) licence.

Apprentices are stationed at Oscoda, though some return to the company's facilities located in other states once they have completed the programme.

The Boeing 747 was the first type of aircraft Kate worked on, to date she has also worked on Boeing 777s operated by Kalitta and Boeing 737s operated by other companies.

When the author spoke with Kate, she was working on a 747 undergoing a heavy maintenance D-check which is performed every six years.

Describing the types of activity involved in a D-check, she said: "We work on the engines, checking the oil filters, hydraulic fluid filters, air filters, we drop the engines if need be. For the structural element, I've completed repairs on the engine pylon. We also remove the interior of the plane, the panels, and the insulation. For the AVI element we inspect wires to ensure there's no chafing and that no clamps are broken. With the interior panels removed we check for corrosion on the inner lining of the aircraft and conduct an NDT inspection to check for cracks in the metal components, this is generally done by our structures division."

The company's goal for completing a D-check is under 58 days, though one aircraft was recently completed in 45 days.

> **"Apprentices are stationed at Oscoda, though some return to the company's facilities located in other states once they have completed the programme."**

Mechanic

Kate Baughman is an apprentice mechanic with Kalitta Air. In this short story she shares her experiences of working on 747 freighter aircraft.

Kalitta Air

Kate said she finds the 747 a lot easier to work on than some types because of its size: "You have more room for situations during AVI when you're checking the wires to make sure there's no chafing so it's easier compared to a smaller 737 in which everything is crammed together."

In terms of the most challenging maintenance task required on a 747 D-check, Kate nominated checking the forward APU bay where the ball screw is: "Nobody likes to go in there because it's awkward to get up to and you've got to get in there and do it but they're very tight spaces.

"Our fuel cell division people climb up and get inside the fuel tanks to undertake inspections and the NDT division conducts its inspections. If any corrosion is found, we go in, remove it, and fix it."

For readers unfamiliar with Oscoda Airport, it's the former Wurtsmith Air Force Base part of Strategic Air Command and home to the 379th Bomb Wing operating B-52 bombers and KC-135 tankers. It's located in upstate Michigan not far from the shore of Lake Huron. During the winter months it gets cold which presents a challenge to those working on aircraft parked on the ramp. Explaining, Kate said: "We have line maintenance folks who tend to work outside most of the time. Heavy maintenance is only conducted inside one of the hangars, but as an aircraft is being prepared to leave it's parked outside on the ramp, so I have to work outside on those occasions. We recently launched a 777 when it was so cold that the water lines were freezing up, so my team and I had to go outside to get the water lines working again. We bundle up and go inside to get warmed up if needed."

Discussing the Kalitta apprenticeship programme, Kate said: "We attend the training

facility where instructors teach us the basics that we need to know before we start working on the shop floor. Throughout the programme we spend time in the various maintenance divisions. Each time we move to a new division such as sheet metal we take a two-week course, that gives us a rundown of what sheet metal is about and how to do it. The training centre gives us the hands-on learning required and ensures we are being taught correctly. We also have on-the-job trainers working with us on the shop floor. My work is issued to me by a maintenance supervisor."

During the remaining 12 months of her programme Kate is moving to the engine shop to learn how to dismantle and rebuild engines, then she'll move to the composites division to learn how to maintain and repair composite components.

"For my A&P licence, I won't take any tests until the very end. But we are tested on our knowledge as we go through the programme, just to make sure we have taken something from it. But the maintenance department does not do that, your maintenance department evaluation grade is based on the judgements of our leading hands and supervisors."

Speaking about the 747 aircraft, Kate said each one is unique. "Each bird has its own thing but, in my opinion, the 747 is a lot easier to troubleshoot," she revealed. "The 777 pretty much tells you what's wrong with it but there's still a lot of bugs, it's too finicky. If you do something wrong, you can blow a fire bottle. With the 747, you really have to mess up in order to hurt the aircraft."

Once a 747 has arrived for its D-check it goes into what's known as pre-dock as Kate explained: "In pre-dock we go through the maintenance requirements based on the cards that are already written up. This means checking the functionality of the aircraft and then troubleshoot from there, to see what's wrong. Pre-dock is followed by a wash day when we wash the aircraft and get it ready to enter the dock inside the hangar where the work starts. The aircraft remains in the same dock for the duration of its check.

"The aircraft's programme of work is split into phases. The project manager is the person who figures out ahead of time, before we even get our pre dock stuff, the first priority tasks for us to get done and then we weed out the rest after that."

When Kate clocks on for a shift she works with over 60 people from the various divisions, one each for the engines, the interior, the flaps, tail, avionics, and sheet metal. The are three different shifts so a lot of people work on the aircraft during the same period.

In addition to the maintenance activities conducted on Kalitta's own fleet of Boeing 747 and 777 freighters, the company offers maintenance services to other aircraft operators on a traditional maintenance, repair, and overhaul basis. The company has a powerplant division, one devoted to air frames, and one to engineering.

POWERPLANT DIVISION

The powerplant division offers a complete range of maintenance services for various engines: the General Electric CF6-80C2, CFM56-3 and CFM56-7 series, the GE90-115B (line-based only), and the Pratt & Whitney PW4000 with the 94in chord engines. Engine testing is also available at the company's 30ft test cell facility. The powerplant division undertakes scheduled on-site maintenance, quick response aircraft on ground situations and remain available for dispatch around the clock.

AIR FRAME SERVICES

A repair station holds a Federal Aviation Administration certificate issued under Title 14 of the Code of Federal Regulations Part 145 comprising hangars and back shop facilities to enable heavy checks, major overhauls, and repairs. Air frame services offers line maintenance assistance and specialises in quick response to aircraft-on-ground (AOG) situations, ones that prevent an aircraft from flying. In addition to its maintenance outstations at Los Angeles, New York-JFK, Cincinnati, Anchorage and Honolulu, personnel travel to any location in support of a customer's AOG situation.

Specialising in the repair of Boeing and McDonnell Douglas aircraft, air frame services can undertake scheduled A, B, C, and D-checks; major structural inspections and repairs, modifications on airframe and powerplant systems; structural and avionics conversions, modifications, and supplemental type certificate installations; cabin modification of passenger and cargo aircraft; aircraft weighing and balance; flight

> "Each bird has its own thing but, in my opinion, the 747 is a lot easier to troubleshoot."

Kalitta Air

Kalitta Air

Kalitta Air

SJIII 4626

control balancing; paint preparation and full exterior painting; and non-destructive testing including fluorescent penetrant, eddy current, ultrasonic, radiographic and magnetic particle.

ENGINEERING

The engineering department, which operates as part of the maintenance division, provides technical support and design capability to all company departments. It offers aircraft structural repair for repairs required beyond published limits that are approved or accepted by the Federal Aviation Administration; modification or alteration design that can be either Federal Aviation Administration approved or accepted to the operators specification; damage tolerance evaluation of previously installed repairs, alterations, or modifications; assistance with or the development of supplemental type certificates to requested configuration; and the development and approval of part manufacturing authorisation for parts requested by a customer.

"When Kate clocks on for a shift she works with over 60 people from the various divisions, one each for the engines, the interior, the flaps, tail, avionics, and sheet metal."

Kalitta Air

A Cargolux Boeing 747-8F undergoing a check in one of the company's hangars at its Luxembourg base. *Cargolux*

Freighter Maintenance

Cargolux Airlines has its own maintenance and engineering division based at Luxembourg led by Ingi Johannessen. He provided insight into the work required to maintain 30 Boeing 747 freighters.

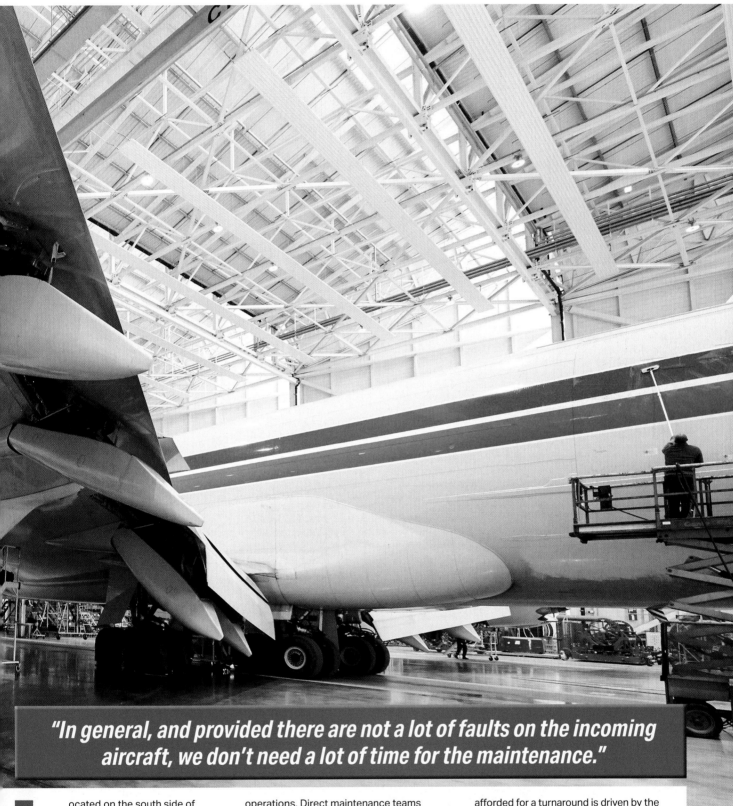

"In general, and provided there are not a lot of faults on the incoming aircraft, we don't need a lot of time for the maintenance."

ocated on the south side of Luxembourg airport, Cargolux's maintenance and engineering division is based in a two-bay hangar spacious enough to house two Boeing 747s. There are a variety of workshops located within the building, one that's a landmark in the small European nation. Workshop capability includes dedicated component work and general fleet maintenance support such as specialised emergency backup for line and hangar operations. Direct maintenance teams work on the line, in the hangar and in the workshops complemented by licensed engineers, all supported by colleagues working in material management, shipping receiving, and technical records.

Discussing hands-on maintenance work undertaken, Ingi Johannessen, vice president of maintenance and engineering with Cargolux said: "We operate the 747-400 and the 747-8 the same way. When they return to our home base here in Luxembourg, we do the between-flight turnarounds or line maintenance, and heavier A-, C-checks. The amount of time afforded for a turnaround is driven by the scheduler, but in general, and provided there are not a lot of faults on the incoming aircraft, we don't need a lot of time for the

BOEING 747 CHECKS		
Check	747-400	747-8
A-check	1,000 hours	1,200 hours
C-check	24 months	32 months
D1-check	6 years	8 years
D2-check	6 years	8 years

Mechanics perform inspections on a GE Aerospace GEnx-2B engine during checks at Cargolux's Luxembourg base. *Cargolux*

maintenance. Line maintenance involves interrogating the aircraft's maintenance computer to see if there are any faults, checking the tyres and fluid levels, and completing a walk around.

"Before A- or C-checks you need to prepare the aircraft by getting everything ready, including primarily, the work package which is based on your maintenance programme to include component changes, mandatory modifications, and extra items. It involves a lot of planning with estimates made for tools, materials, and manpower required which enables you to plan the check and sequence the tasks.

"We start by conducting what's known as pre-hangar work, so we prepare the aircraft, establish the correct fuel levels, complete specific ground checks and certain functional checks which are part of the maintenance programme and verify any faults, undertake fault rectification, and you might do the first inspections. What's most important is to get the aircraft into the hangar, prepared and secured so the people can start to work on it. You might have to jack it, you need to secure

the landing gear doors and lock them, you might need to secure the flight controls in case somebody puts hydraulic power on and ensure the moving surfaces don't move, and to enable inspections, you must open access panels or create access.

"We don't do our own D-checks, that work is outsourced to MROs in China and Taiwan. That said, we know the D-check process which typically involves opening-up the aircraft. Much of the work undertaken for a D-check depends on your inspection package. With an older aircraft you might have to strip it completely removing for example the floors and the sidewall panels and remove insulation blankets under the panels so you can inspect the aircraft's structural components. Zonal inspections are generally visual and depending on the system or the structure or the criticality of the structure or what has been certified in the maintenance programme, you might go into deeper levels of inspection, either a detailed visual inspection or by one or a combination of non-destructive tests."

Non-destructive testing (NDT) detects and evaluates flaws in a material. NDT technicians

can choose from a range of techniques, one of which is called eddy-current testing. This is a sub-surface technique that induces an electromagnetic field in an object and measures the secondary magnetic field generated around the electric current to determine where flaws are within that object. When used in aircraft maintenance, the technique will detect cracks caused by fatigue or corrosion.

Providing insight to more D-check events, Ingi said: "You might need to test the fuel system or the valves and the pumps. The fuel tank itself is a structural element so you might need to conduct structural inspections inside the fuel tanks, do visual checks of the sealant and a perform leak check. Inspection of the bonding features of the fuel tank systems are critical to verify that there is no risk of electrical arcing. A lot of modifications to the fuel system and inspections were added to the D-check because of the investigations into the loss of a TWA 747 off Long Island, New York on July 17, 1996.

"There's also a lot of inspections, especially on the 400, of the flight controls, carriages,

Engine cowlings opened on a GE Aerospace GEnx-2B engine during a major check. *Cargolux*

Opened in May 2009, Cargolux's maintenance hangar is 656ft (200m) wide, 295ft (90m) deep and 138ft (42m) high. It has two work bays, each capable of housing a Boeing 747-8F during maintenance. *Cargolux*

> **"Freight is Cargolux's bread and butter, so the loading systems, primarily the nose door and the side doors, on its aircraft are crucial to its operations."**

linkages, bearings, and rollers. The motors are pretty much on condition so even during a D-check you might replace some, but otherwise you leave them on condition. Flaps and ailerons are inspected for damage and delamination. At the end of the inspection process, you conduct functional checks by moving the flight control surfaces up and down. The 400 and the -8 have completely different flap systems. The 747-400 has a triple-slotted flap system comprising a fore flap, a mid-flap, and an aft flap. The 747-8 has a double-slotted flap system comprising a fore flap and a main flap. The components are bigger and heavier, but the mechanisms are simplified.

"The landing gears are just serviced and inspected during an A-check because the landing gears are on a 10-year interval. So, during a D-check at eight years, the landing gear still has two years of life remaining, so we schedule the landing gear changes independently of the D-check. Given there were fewer 747-8 aircraft built, the availability of landing gears is more critical, so we try

to optimise the intervals. So, we schedule a landing gear change in the next C-check after the first D-check and thereby maximise the use of the landing gears. Due to scheduling and availability of gears we have had to change some gears at eight years during a D-check. Generally, a D-check will include functional checks and a visual inspection of the landing gears. Depending on the work being undertaken for a D-check, there could be some tasks required on the gear or on the

landing gear doors that require a gear swing to enable adjustments to be made if required, but typically we don't do a gear swing. The landing gear is next cycled during the aircraft's test flight immediately after the D-check is complete."

Freight is Cargolux's bread and butter, so the loading systems, primarily the nose door and the side doors, on its aircraft are crucial to its operations. Surprisingly, there's little by the way of requirements for maintaining the loading systems in Boeing's maintenance programme because it's not a safety critical system. Typically, the operators devise a maintenance programme of their own. Ingi said Cargolux removes the whole system at every C- and D-check, cleans and inspects all the parts and performs thorough maintenance.

Engine maintenance is integrated into the aircraft maintenance programme, so when it's in the hangar, the same mechanic works on the engine as on the aircraft, the work is all planned together. Engine issues are identified using a health monitoring system. Mechanics consult the manufacturer for support, and

Mechanics remove the fan case on a large turbofan engine. *Cargolux*

when an engine is removed, typically it is returned to the manufacturer.

Surprisingly, there's not maintenance done on the flight deck during a C- or D-check but panels are removed to access structural components that need inspection but are positioned behind the panels. According to Ingi: "At the end of the check, you run ground and functional checks from the flight deck and take the opportunity to clean the flight deck and restore worn carpets and panels."

Highlighting some notable aspects of the various checks, Ingi said: "The D2-check involves more inspections carried out in accordance with the Supplemental Structural Inspection Document, which are related to the aircraft's age. The number of man hours required for checks on our 400-series aircraft are getting much heavier because the aircraft are getting old. We complete a C-check for a 747-8 in a week, but if it includes a landing gear change it will take a little over two weeks, compared to a typical 747-400 C-check which takes three weeks."

Discussing the quantity of 747 checks completed by the Cargolux maintenance and engineering division, Ingi said: "We do between 100 and 128 checks a year. Outsourced D-check work is done by companies that are certified with all the required approvals and quality systems. We send a team of highly qualified mechanics and inspectors to monitor the progress of the checks and the standard of quality being upheld. We plan our schedule of checks to suit our operations. Individual aircraft are flown from the airport where the revenue earning route concluded direct to the MRO, and after completion of its check the aircraft is entered straight back into service. Most of the

MROs we use are located at places where the company conducts cargo operations so once the maintenance work is complete, we load the aircraft and fly away with revenue-earning cargo onboard, though that's not always possible. Otherwise, we ferry the aircraft to the nearest airport that we're operating freight from.

"From a maintenance perspective, the engines, and the flight control surfaces between a 747-400 and a 747-8 are completely different. Cargolux was the launch customer for the 747-8 and therefore the GE Aerospace GEnx-2B engine. We suffered many teething problems and a high number of removals. With very good support and help provided by the engine manufacturer, we've been able to improve that, but there are still inspections that are required on the engine that can result in an engine removal. The

747-8 is equipped with different flight control surfaces compared to a 400, so we have had to learn how to handle and service them."

Cargolux also had to deal with structural issues on the 747-8, specifically cracks in specific stringers, common to the end fittings on the aft side of the bulkhead at station. Following an investigation, Boeing discovered that during assembly un-shimmed or incorrectly shimmed gaps were larger than engineering requirements. This caused excessive and sustained internal tensile stresses and resulted in stress corrosion cracking in the stringers. Consequently, the Federal Aviation Administration issued a directive, requiring operators of all Boeing 747-8I and Boeing 747-8F aircraft to complete detailed inspections for cracks and on-condition actions.

Boeing 747-8F LX-VCL inside the gargantuan maintenance hangar where Cargolux conducts all its A- and C-checks. Cargolux

Loading Ops

Between them, Eric Reisch and Paul Hoffman manage load control and operations for Cargolux Airlines. They provided the editor with an overview of insight handling and managing the operator's cargo operations.

Eric Reisch is Cargolux's senior manager for load control and ramp and up-steering operations with responsibility for managing the company's 30 loadmasters. His responsibility in up-steering involves compiling information from various departments, such as the warehouse, fuelling, and flight operations, to enable an understanding of any issues that may be faced during a day.

Paul Hoffman is responsible for operations at Cargolux and the director of ground engineering with responsibility for calculations about how to spread the weight onto the aircraft floor, lashing and restraining in support of special, heavy, and off-size cargo.

Explaining his role, Paul said: "My job comprises three different parts. One, to ensure that we have the right procedures to load and offload cargo, to fuel the aircraft, and to ensure we have the servicing and ground operations capability to support our 747 aircraft. Two, to ensure all our loadmasters are trained to acceptable standards. And three, to manage special cargo operations for which the 747 provides heavy load capacity, and the ability to load using the nose door. We need to palletise our loads on ULDs [for details of ULDs

Cargolux Boeing 747 Freighters have two cargo holds, one each in the belly and on the main deck. Key Collection

Airlifting outsized cargo is one specialised service offered by Cargolux. One benefit of the Boeing 747-8F is the aircraft's nose cargo door, which eases the loading of long objects. Christophe Van Biesen

please see the section titled Unit Load Devices] to ensure that the load is shored, restrained, and distributed properly, then we move the ULD onboard the aircraft. A 20ft pallet can carry up to 28 tonnes. The 747 will carry incredibly high loads."

FREIGHT OPERATIONS

Outlining the freight operations undertaken by Cargolux at Luxembourg, Eric said: "Our operations are straightforward because we operate a single-type fleet. Paul's department runs the technical calculations and gains approval before the job is passed to me in operations. At Luxembourg, we turn around 100 flights per week, so that's 100 export flights and 100 import flights per week. Depending on where they come from, many of them have special loads onboard and standard size containers and pallets which are easy to handle.

"After arriving at our facility, the pallets are offloaded from the truck, transferred through the warehouse, and then weighed. Once those procedures are completed, we do our weight and balance for the aircraft. Depending on the route, we plan cargo in the most efficient way to prevent losing time during stops on the route because we don't necessarily operate with one destination. We work with a flight commitment, a booking list which has a deadline. For us to meet that deadline, all the processes within the logistics chain, exports, customs, need to run smoothly to build-up the cargo on pallets ready to be loaded.

"Due to the complexity of the load, the loadmaster has input to the flight's cargo build up at an early stage to ensure that we spread the load and stay within the limit, and re-check feasibility based on the actual nature and size of the cargo. The loadmaster also checks the temperature control because we must avoid temperature conflict at the loading stage. At the planning stage we need to ensure awareness on what the segregations are and where to position which loads in the most efficient way. Each of our loadmasters is certified as a load planner and a loading supervisor on each variant of a 747 we operate and undertakes periodic refresher training. That means they can plan the flight and have someone else load the flight or they can plan and load the flight themselves. The loadmaster flies with the load to its destination, but for destinations not served by a regular flight, the support required for offloading may not meet requirements, so we take other people to help with the offload.

Groundcrew cargo inside the belly hold of Boeing 747-8R7F LX-VCC (c/n 35807) at Luxembourg Airport. Cargolux

"We have a work schedule, which remains flexible, so that we can accommodate the peak times throughout the week. Certain days will be more challenging than others. On one day you may have 12 departures, on another day you may have 20, so we strive to accommodate the peaks and remain flexible enough to overcome the problems that you may encounter during the day of operation. We try to utilise the 400s and the 8s in the most efficient way. Because the -8 is more fuel efficient, we tend to use it on longer routes."

BOEING 747-400, BOEING 747-8

Commenting on the differences between a 400 and an 8, Paul said: "For a loadmaster, the difference between the 400 and the 8 is small. That's because Boeing used a common approach in designing and building all its freighter types. The loading and restraining systems only differ based on the tweaks implemented to optimise the systems on each type. But the basic philosophy behind the usage of the system is almost identical. The 8 has more pallet positions compared to a 400 because it has a longer fuselage and therefore more capacity. And its environmental control system was substantially upgraded, the new air conditioning packs perform better."

Explaining, Eric said: "It's a standard system with an ambient temperature range between 2°C and 29°C which meets the main IATA temperature categorisations, 2°C to 8°C and 15°C to 25°C, without any problem. Any temperature requirement below the range needs active or passive containers to be used, either dry ice or electric containers that cool down to -30°C. We run a temperature feasibility from origin to destination based on the customer's needs. At what temperature will you need to pick up the goods or will they be delivered under temperature control to our facilities in Luxembourg where we have a dedicated farming area, where we have dedicated cooling centres to handle the goods. The distance from the cooling centre out to the aircraft at Luxembourg is about 100 metres so the transfer from the facility to the aircraft is timely and efficient. We have 12 dedicated cargo spots at the Luxembourg Airport cargo centre upon which we can handle an aircraft, and up to six aircraft simultaneously. Competitors also operate from the cargo centre, but Cargolux is the operator with the largest presence because it's our home base and we also have our maintenance facility setup at the airport."

SPECIAL CARGO

Providing some examples of special cargo flown by Cargolux, Paul said: "We often carry oil drilling equipment, and MRI scanners for hospitals. The customer sends us a request for transportation of a specific shipment.

Simultaneous loading of a Boeing 747-8F via the upper deck cargo door (left side) and the lower deck cargo door (right side). Cargolux

We analyse technical drawings, technical information, and photos from the customer to determine how to spread the load onto the aircraft floor. This involves checking the support structure and comparing the information with the aircraft's limitations. We then check if there are any special restrictions that might apply because of the commodity itself. For instance, if you have liquid cargo or a crated item or one that is shock sensitive, we must check how to accommodate the requirements of the cargo and the needs of the aircraft. If you are planning to carry a liquid cargo you must be careful to minimise sloshing which can start sudden oscillations which can cause the aircraft to start to shake."

Securing a cargo within the aircraft to its specific needs is another procedure that must be done with great care. For example, the largest Siemens MRI scanner carried by Cargolux weighed 25 tonnes. Explaining, Eric said: "Planning to carry the 25-tonne MRI scanner involved a collaborative effort between Siemens and Paul's department to design the frame that would spread the load

over the 20ft pallet footprint, and to ensure the machinery is loadable through the side cargo doors. The 747's outside cargo door, floor load limit, and temperature control made the aircraft compatible with the load. The MRI scanner was transported by truck from Siemens Magnet Technology in Oxford to Luxembourg, then loaded by crane on to the pallet."

Another example of special cargo involved the transportation of a 37m long piece of equipment for a freeport liquid natural gas terminal on a charter shipment from Pattaya, Thailand to Houston, Texas. The shipment involved the handling and transport of outsized piping units which required bespoke handling and transport conditions. The scope of the project called for multiple flights.

Cargolux's charter department worked with Paul's ground engineering department and its dedicated special cargo analysing function to ensure the feasibility of carrying the loads on a 747 and to determine the exact requirements for the flight. Once the project was deemed

possible for the team, the next issue to be determined was the capability of Pattaya Airport to handle a 747 freighter.

Initially, Bangkok Airport was reluctant to facilitate the operation, given the complexity and space required on the tarmac. But after an Antonov flight also chartered for the project got cleared to depart from Pattaya Airport, a Cargolux team was sent to Pattaya to discuss options. For Cargolux, Pattaya Airport was a new location and one that does not normally operate cargo. The operation was carefully planned and involved four 747 charter flights from Pattaya to Houston, Texas. Two loadmasters, an engineer, a charter manager and several Cargolux colleagues from Bangkok were required on site for the first two flights to ensure the operation ran smoothly. The project was successfully completed, and the equipment was safely flown to Houston.

UNIT LOAD DEVICES
According to the International Air Transport Association (IATA) a unit load device (ULD) is either an aircraft pallet and pallet net combination, or an aircraft container.

ULDs are removable aircraft parts subject to strict civil aviation authorities' requirements from design, testing, production, and operations, to repair and maintenance. An airworthy ULD must be structurally capable of restraining the loads and providing adequate protection to the aircraft systems and structure during flight.

ULDs are the only aircraft parts that leave the control of the airline, return after passing through many unregulated hands, and have an impact on flight safety. As most ULD operations are outsourced to ground service providers, together with the increasing demands for shipper built ULDs from shippers and freight forwarders, it has become critically challenging for airlines to control and supervise the safety compliance in ULD operations.

ULDs are divided into two types: Pallets and Containers. Pallets are secured by a net, attached to the rim of the pallet. The final shape (contour) chosen in the build-up of a ULD needs to fit the allocated aircraft type. Pallets are used if the cargo is difficult to fit into containers, if there are more options for build-up, or when a pallet is the only way to

Cargolux operates 14 747-8 Freighters, including LX-VCB. Boeing

carry special load cargo. The alternative to a pallet is a container which provides the shape (contour). The contents are secured either by closing and bolting the doors, or by securing the door net to the rims of the container walls and floor. A container is faster to load/unload and provides the cargo with better protection against damage and weather conditions.

In general, ULDs are owned by airlines so the respective handling agents must maintain a regular stock check. Both the airline and its agent must complete a UCR (ULD Control Receipt) when releasing or accepting ULDs: a vital document for determining responsibility and liability for the release and acceptance process.

Contours (the overall shape) are created for the build-up of open pallet ULDs with consideration and adherence given to the routing, the type of recipient aircraft, and its loading position on that aircraft. ULD contours take account of the structural dimensions of the recipient aircraft to be loaded.

Standard form ULDs tend to fit on most types of aircraft and in most positions, other types of aircraft require non-standard sized ULDs, especially for specific positions, with the correct contour. Before build-up begins, the maximum loading capacity of the aircraft type and the ULD must be confirmed.

For cargo that requires special handling, both the handling agent and the airline must take precautions that protect the cargo, the aircraft, handling personnel, and accompanying consignments. Priority handling is necessary for urgent cargo.

TIE-DOWN

When securing cargo loaded on a pallet, the base is covered with plastic sheeting, and the load shaped to the correct contour for its loading position on the aircraft. A plastic sheet is used to cover the load and give protection against the elements. The net used to secure the load is checked for serviceability and placed over the consignment covering all packages.

Before tensioning the net, fittings are attached and evenly spread out. Corner lashings tighten the load down in accordance with the contents: straps should be tensioned without damaging the cargo or bending the pallet.

A serviceable net used on the main cargo deck must withstand a 15,000lb loading.

Note the lights inside the nose door to provide illumination of the loading area. Cargolux

A container (on the right) and a pallet (to the left) sat on a Trepel high-loader prior to loading on board Boeing 747-8F LX-VCI. Cargolux

A dramatic night-time photo of a Cargolux Boeing 747 freighter at Milan Airport. The aircraft is being simultaneously loaded with pallets from high loaders to the lower deck (left side) and the upper deck (right side). An air stair is parked to the upper deck crew door. Cargolux

When placing cargo in a container, it must be loaded in a way that it will not fall out when the door is open. Containers fitted with a flexible door must be loaded in a way that avoids the packages pressing against the plastic door or deforming the container's contour.

Additional tie downs, lashing or strapping may be required for special loads or unusual consignments such as aircraft engines, cars, and some machinery, dependent on its weight and the capacity of the tie downs, lashing and strapping being used.

Tie down attachment points must be spaced evenly to allow maximum effectiveness, at a minimum 10in from the corner of the pallet.

By spreading the weight of the load over as much of the surface area available in a pallet or container it is more secure and facilitates easier loading, an even weight and balance of the aircraft, and avoids damaging the aircraft's structure.

IDENTIFICATION

Once a ULD is built up and complete, to make it available and acceptable for loading on the aircraft

Pallets loaded with boxes of flowers being towed to the loader for loading on board a now long-retired Boeing 747-100 freighter. Cargolux

The Cargolux livery features a tail marking featuring three stylised cargo boxes. Cargolux

it must have a ULD tag listing all the information required by ramp agents. Before loading on the aircraft, the information is cross-referenced with the flight documentation at the aircraft.

To load the aircraft correctly, the ULD tag must list the following information: correct tag for the consignments loaded on/in the ULD; a ULD number; its destination, gross weight and airline, and a signature stating the ULD is correctly built, and the weight correctly established.

The ramp agent must ensure the ULD is not overweight for its loading position on the aircraft position and is within the maximum gross weight for the type of ULD.

The tag is affixed on the long side of the pallet by wire fasteners or in a pocket on container door to ease the information cross-checking, a process completed before being unloaded from the K-loader or truck. A discrepancy may deem the ULD non-compliant for loading such that it's returned to the handling company for rectification.

DANGEROUS GOODS
Commodities that possess potentially hazardous characteristics are deemed as dangerous goods and require stringent precautions for transportation onboard an aircraft. Dangerous goods range from acids, through radioactive materials, to aerosol sprays, and bleach.

Technical instructions for the safe transportation of dangerous goods by aircraft issued by IATA contain internationally agreed rules and the procedures that must be followed by all personnel involved for preparing each consignment and loading it/them on an aircraft.

Dangerous goods are divided into four categories: acceptable, forbidden, forbidden but exempted by those states involved in the flight plan, and excepted.

A line of five Cargolux Boeing 747-200 freighters parked on loading spots at the Luxair cargo centre at Luxembourg Airport. Cargolux